# The Twelve Days of Christmas

## Kent Merrell

# THE TWELVE DAYS OF CHRISTMAS

*The Twelve Most Important Days in the*

*Life of the Savior, Jesus Christ*



This book is a work of personal reflection and religious interpretation. The selection and discussion of the "twelve days" represent the author's individual views and spiritual insights, not an official doctrine or exhaustive list. The author makes no claims of infallibility and encourages readers to seek personal revelation and study the scriptures. And as mentioned, the author appreciates the great work gleaned from the many great scholars quoted and referenced herein. Thus for those quoted or referenced the author hopes he got it right.

Current Edition Published 2026

ISBN: 979-8-9903523-7-7 (print)

ISBN: 979-8-9903523-8-4 (ebook)


And by the way:

The Traditional English Carol lyrics and melody of The Twelve Days of Christmas are in the public domain worldwide, with the words first published in England c. 1780 and the now-standard tune popularized by Frederic Austin's 1909 arrangement (now also in the public domain in the United States and most jurisdictions).

# Note on Sources and Voices Referenced

It has been more than a decade since I first wrote The Twelve Days of Christmas. Though I have received many requests to republish it, I hesitated for one reason: during my initial writing and research, I did not fully credit the many authors, scholars, and inspired leaders whose words and insights shaped my understanding. It would be unfair to accept praise for wisdom that rightly belongs to others.

In this renewed edition, I have made a sincere effort to identify and attribute the origin of the teachings, concepts, and quotations that influenced this work. Technology and further study have assisted me in tracing many of these sources. If you recognize a passage or idea that I have not properly attributed—or have attributed incorrectly—I welcome your correction and will gratefully amend it. The last thing I desire is for any reader to assume that any profound truth presented here originates with me alone.

With gratitude to those who have taught, written, testified, and illuminated the life of the Savior, I acknowledge the following foundational sources.

## The Standard Works (Primary Scriptural Sources)

The majority of references in this book come from what members of The Church of Jesus Christ of Latter-day Saints call the Standard Works—four volumes of holy scripture written by prophets across the centuries. These include the King James Version of the Bible, the Book of Mormon, the Doctrine and Covenants, and the Pearl of Great Price. All are available online in full at: https://www.churchofjesuschrist.org/study/scriptures?lang=eng

### (KJV) — King James Version of the Bible

The King James Version, first published in 1611 under the direction of King James I, is the classic English translation of the Bible, containing 39 books of the Old Testament and 27 books of the New Testament.

### (BOM) — The Book of Mormon: Another Testament of Jesus Christ

A sacred record of God's dealings with ancient inhabitants of the Americas, written by prophets and translated by revelation through Joseph Smith from golden plates first published in 1830. It begins with a family leaving Jerusalem around 600 B.C. and concludes about A.D. 421.

**Books of the Book of Mormon Referenced:** 1 Nephi; 2 Nephi; Jacob; Enos; Jarom; Omni; Words of Mormon (WoM); Mosiah; Alma; Helaman; 3 Nephi; 4 Nephi; Mormon; Ether; Moroni.

**(D&C) — Doctrine and Covenants**

A collection of 138 revealed sections given to modern prophets regarding the restoration of the Church of Jesus Christ of Latter-day Saints. Each section contains inspired instruction and doctrine for the latter days.

**(PGP) — Pearl of Great Price** - A volume of scripture containing:

>**The Book of Moses** – Revelations to Joseph Smith concerning the Creation and early prophets.
>
>**The Book of Abraham** – Translations from ancient papyri revealing Abraham's visions and teachings.
>
>**Joseph Smith—History (JS—H)** – Joseph Smith's account of his First Vision and early prophetic calling.
>
>**Articles of Faith** – Thirteen concise statements summarizing core beliefs.
>
>**(JST) — Joseph Smith Translation of the Bible** - Inspired revisions and clarifications to the biblical text made by the Prophet Joseph Smith to restore plain and precious truths.

## Additional Foundational Works Frequently Referenced

**Jesus the Christ — James E. Talmage (1915)** - A doctrinal and scriptural study of the life and ministry of Jesus Christ, widely respected among Latter-day Saint readers.

**Teachings of the Prophet Joseph Smith (Compiled 1938)** - A compilation of sermons and teachings of Joseph Smith, edited primarily by Joseph Fielding Smith.

**Doctrines of Salvation — Joseph Fielding Smith (1954, Vols. 1–3)** - A comprehensive doctrinal work explaining numerous gospel principles and teachings.

Journal of Discourses

A historical compilation of sermons delivered by early leaders of the Church; valuable for historical insight and doctrinal development, though some teachings reflect the context of their time.

Ensign Magazine

The official monthly magazine of the Church (published from 1971–2020), containing General Conference addresses, doctrinal articles, and inspirational messages. Conference talks and articles are available online at: https://www.churchofjesuschrist.org/study/magazines?lang=eng

## About many of the Voices Referenced in This Book

The following individuals are quoted or referenced for their teachings, scholarship, testimony, or scriptural authorship. Brief descriptions are provided to help readers understand their background and contribution.

**James E. Talmage** – Apostle and theologian best known for Jesus the Christ, a doctrinal study of the Savior's life and mission.

**Joseph Smith** – Prophet of the Restoration through whom modern revelation and additional scripture were brought forth.

**John Taylor** – Third President of the Church and author of Mediation and Atonement, a doctrinal exposition of Christ's redeeming role.

**Brigham Young** – Second President of the Church who led the Latter-day Saints to the Salt Lake Valley and taught extensively on gospel doctrine.

**Joseph Fielding Smith** – Tenth President of the Church and prolific doctrinal writer, author of Doctrines of Salvation.

**Russell M. Nelson** – Seventeenth President of the Church, former heart surgeon, and teacher emphasizing the doctrine of the body, creation, and covenant discipleship.

**Henry B. Eyring** – Counselor in the First Presidency, noted for thoughtful spiritual instruction and reflections on faith and revelation.

**Donald Q. Cannon** – Historian and scholar focused on early Restoration teachings and the life of Joseph Smith.

**Larry E. Dahl** – Professor of ancient scripture at Brigham Young University and co-author of scholarly works on Restoration theology.

**John W. Welch** – Legal scholar and founder of FARMS, known for research on chiasmus and ancient literary forms in scripture.

**Andrew C. Skinner** – Scholar of ancient scripture and the Book of Abraham, noted for educational and devotional writings.

**William Clayton** – Early Church leader and personal secretary to Joseph Smith whose journals preserve key historical teachings.

**E. A. Wallis Budge** – British Egyptologist whose translations made many ancient Near Eastern and Christian texts accessible to modern readers.

**Timothy, Archbishop of Alexandria** – Early Christian leader whose writings reflect ancient theological thought on creation and redemption.

**Moses** – Old Testament prophet and lawgiver traditionally credited with leading Israel from Egypt and recording foundational teachings on Creation and the Fall.

**Abraham** – Patriarch-prophet whose covenant and visions form a central foundation of biblical and Restoration theology.

**Nephi** – Book of Mormon prophet-historian whose writings testify of Jesus Christ and the future Restoration.

**Enoch** – Ancient prophet who established a Zion people so righteous that they were taken into God's presence.

**Noah** – Old Testament prophet called to preserve life through the Flood and exemplify obedience amid widespread wickedness.

With deep gratitude to these scriptural authors, prophets, scholars, and witnesses whose insights have enriched my understanding of the Savior's life, I offer this work as a personal devotional reflection rather than a claim of original scholarship.

# Forward

When most people hear The Twelve Days of Christmas, they picture turtle doves, golden rings, and partridges in pear trees. But for me, the twelve days of Christmas are not about gifts or festive traditions—they are about the life and mission of my Savior, Jesus Christ.

A few years ago, as I was preparing to teach a Christmas lesson for the Sunday before Christmas Day, the familiar tune of The Twelve Days of Christmas kept running through my mind. But instead of doves and drummers drumming, I thought of Courts on High, Humble Mangers, and Sacred Groves. The lesson took on a new meaning. Rather than counting down twelve days of worldly materialism leading up to a commercial holiday, I saw it as an opportunity to reflect on the twelve most significant days in Christ's life—the twelve days that shaped my faith, my understanding, and my personal salvation.

Of course, choosing only twelve was no easy task. The Savior's life is filled with moments of divine power, mercy, and sacrifice. But since it was my lesson to teach, I made my own selection—twelve days that, to me, represent the most profound and pivotal events in His earthly ministry. You might choose twelve entirely different days, and that's fine. In fact, I suspect we'd agree on a few, such as His Birth, Crucifixion, and Resurrection. But my hope is that as I share my twelve, even if you would have chosen differently, you will understand why these moments mean so much to me.

One thing that guided my selection was a simple but sincere question: *Lord, which days were Your big days?*

In answer to my question, here's what I found the Savior saying about His days.

When the Savior introduced Himself to the Prophet Joseph Smith, He didn't just state His name—He declared His role in creation, His connection to Enoch, and His sacrifice for all mankind:

> "I am the same which spake, and the world was made, and all
> things came by me. I am the same which have taken the Zion
> of Enoch into mine own bosom; and verily, I say, even as many

as have believed in my name, for I am Christ, and in mine own name, by the virtue of the blood which I have spilt, have I pleaded before the Father for them." (D&C 38:3-4)

When speaking of His Second Coming, Jesus referenced the days of Noah. He made it clear that, just as in Noah's time, people would be caught up in their daily lives, oblivious to the warnings until it was too late:

"But as the days of Noe were, so shall also the coming of the Son of man be. For as in the days that were before the flood they were eating and drinking, marrying and giving in marriage, until the day that Noe entered into the ark." (Matt. 24:37-38)

Luke recorded it this way:

"And as it was in the days of Noe, so shall it be also in the days of the Son of man. They did eat, they drank, they married wives, they were given in marriage, until the day that Noe entered into the ark, and the flood came, and destroyed them all." (Luke 17:26-27)

When the resurrected Savior visited the Americas, He once again testified of His divine role, declaring:

"Behold, I am Jesus Christ the Son of God. I created the heavens and the earth, and all things that in them are. I was with the Father from the beginning. I am in the Father, and the Father in me; and in me hath the Father glorified his name." (3 Nephi 9:15)

He also gave a simple but powerful confirmation of His birth:

"Behold, I am Jesus Christ, whom the prophets testified shall come into the world." (3 Nephi 11:10)

And He spoke of His mission as Redeemer, one that was set in motion long before the world began:

"Behold, I am he who was prepared from the foundation of the world to redeem my people." (Ether 3:14)

The Lord also spoke about Adam and Eve—about the choice they made and its consequences for all humanity:

"But, behold, I say unto you that I, the Lord God, gave unto Adam and unto his seed, that they should not die as to the temporal death, until I, the Lord God, should send forth angels to declare unto them repentance and redemption, through faith on the name of mine Only Begotten Son." (D&C 20:42)

He confirmed His decision to remove Adam and Eve from the Garden:

> "And it came to pass that after I, the Lord God, had driven them
> out, that Adam began to till the earth, and to have dominion over
> all the beasts of the field, and to eat his bread by the sweat of his
> brow, as I the Lord had commanded him. And Eve, also, his wife,
> did labor with him." (Moses 5:1)

Did you notice how many of the Savior's "big days" He personally referenced? His calling in the premortal life, the Creation, the expulsion from Eden, the Flood, the City of Enoch, His earthly ministry, the Atonement, and His Second Coming—all events He Himself spoke about. And in other scriptures, He affirms the rest.

One of my favorite references is when Jesus told His disciples that He had another flock to visit:

> "And other sheep I have, which are not of this fold: them also I
> must bring, and they shall hear my voice." (John 10:16)

Nephi also saw in vision the role of Christ's apostles:

> "And the angel spake unto me, saying: These last records, which
> thou hast seen among the Gentiles, shall establish the truth of
> the first, which are of the twelve apostles of the Lamb." (1 Nephi
> 13:40)

None of these days are insignificant. Each one shaped the course of history and eternity.

When I first taught this lesson that Sunday before Christmas, it quickly became clear that a single forty-minute Sunday School lesson was nowhere near enough time. We barely covered two days, and even those felt rushed. So, on the first Sunday of each month throughout the following year, we took time to explore each one of these significant days in depth.

The "Twelve Days of Christmas" also became a favorite topic in our family discussions. When we visited other families and friends it was difficult to avoid sharing and teaching what I was learning.

Eventually, people began asking me to write down the references and key points. This book is the result—a compilation of my notes and thoughts on The Twelve Most Important Days in the Life of My Savior, Jesus Christ.

1. ____________________________________

2. ____________________________________

3. ____________________________________

4. ____________________________________

5. ____________________________________

6. ____________________________________

7. ____________________________________

8. ____________________________________

9. ____________________________________

10. ____________________________________

11. ____________________________________

12. ____________________________________

# PREFACE

Before diving into The Twelve Days of Christmas, we did something fun in our discussions—I handed out a piece of paper to each person and asked them to write down what they believed were the twelve most important days in the life of the Savior.

So before you read any further, I invite you to do the same. Take a moment, jot down your list, and then see how ours compare. There's no right or wrong answer here—just different perspectives.

Of course, the Savior has had far more than twelve significant days, but these are the ones that have had the deepest impact on me personally. These are the days I feel carry the greatest eternal weight in my own life.

You'll also notice that I've taken some liberties with the definition of "day." I hope you'll forgive me for that.

# The First Day of Christmas

*"Father, thy will be done, and the glory be thine forever."*

## Jesus Ordained of the Father to be the Savior of Mankind.

Jesus Christ accepted the call to serve as my Savior. In doing so, He made the entire Plan of Salvation possible.

> 1 - He defended our free agency.
> 2 – He made it possible for us to become Gods.
> 3 – He introduced us to the plan of salvation.

Jesus set the first example of obedience and submissiveness to His Father. He was meek, humble and willing to take upon Himself the ultimate task, but give the glory back to the Father. We know that even though He was the Firstborn, He had never gone through anything like it and He was totally running on His trust in His Father.

This type of commitment is totally above my head. What I do know is that it took Heavenly Father's endorsement (ordination) of His Son to set in motion the process for justice to be satisfied by mercy. This took place in that grand council and we were there. We chose sides, and our side won. Because of Jesus' great humility and obedience and love, He rallied us to His side. I am forever grateful He did.

*"In that August council of the angels and the Gods, the Being who later was born in flesh as Mary's Son, Jesus, took prominent part, and there was He ordained of the Father to be the Savior of mankind. As to time, the term being used in the sense of all duration past, this is our earliest record of the Firstborn among the sons of God; to us who read, it marks the beginning of the written history of Jesus the Christ."*

Jesus the Christ – James E. Talmage pg. 9

It is almost frightening to think we could have been on Satan's side. I see today people willing to give up their freedom for security and shy away from responsibility. We face the same battle today that we faced in our pre-mortal life. Compare Satan's plan of "sin-free" to the more risky challenge of becoming Godly.

> *"Satan's plan of compulsion, whereby all would be safely conducted through the career of mortality, bereft of freedom to act and agency to choose, so circumscribed that they would be compelled to do right – that one soul would not be lost – was rejected; and the humble offer of Jesus the Firstborn – to assume mortality and live among men as their Exemplar and Teacher, observing the sanctity of man's agency but teaching men to use aright that divine heritage – was accepted. The decision brought war, which resulted in the vanquishment of Satan and his angels, who were cast out and deprived of the boundless privileges incident to the mortal or second estate."*

Jesus the Christ – James E. Talmage pg. 8

The writings of both Moses and Abraham outline this grand event of what I consider the first day of Christmas.

> 1. AND I, the Lord God, spake unto Moses, saying: That Satan, whom thou hast commanded in the name of mine Only Begotten, is the same which was from the beginning, and he came before me, saying—Behold, here am I, send me, I will be thy son, and I will redeem all mankind, that one soul shall not be lost, and surely I will do it; wherefore give me thine honor.

> 2. But, behold, my Beloved Son, which was my Beloved and Chosen from the beginning, said unto me—Father, thy will be done, and the glory be thine forever.

> 3. Wherefore, because that Satan rebelled against me, and sought to destroy the agency of man, which I, the Lord God, had given him, and also, that I should give unto him mine own power; by the power of mine Only Begotten, I caused that he should be cast down;

> 4. And he became Satan, yea, even the devil, the father of all lies, to deceive and to blind men, and to lead them captive at his will, even as many as would not hearken unto my voice.

(Pearl of Great Price | Moses 4:1 - 4)

> 27 And the Lord said: Whom shall I send? And one answered like unto the Son of Man: Here am I, send me. And another answered

and said: Here am I, send me. And the Lord said: I will send the first.

 28 And the second was angry, and kept not his first estate; and, at that day, many followed after him.

(Pearl of Great Price | Abraham 3:27 - 28)

President John Taylor, our third President of the restored Church of Jesus Christ of Latter-day Saints makes the day seem very special because as he puts it – we shouted for joy.

*"It is consistent to believe that at the Council in the heavens the plan that should be adopted in relation to the sons of God who were then spirits, and had not yet obtained tabernacles, was duly considered. For, in view of the creation of the world and the placing of men upon it, whereby it would be possible for them to obtain tabernacles, and in those tabernacles obey laws of life, and with them again be exalted among the Gods we are told that at that time, 'morning stars sang together, and all the sons of God shouted for joy.' The question then arose, how, and upon what principle should the salvation, exaltation and eternal glory of God's sons be brought about? It is evident that at that Council certain plans had been proposed and discussed, and that after a full discussion of those principles, and the declaration of the Father's will pertaining to His design, Lucifer came before the Father with a plan of his own, saying,*

*"AND I, the Lord God, spake unto Moses, saying: That Satan, whom thou hast commanded in the name of mine Only Begotten, is the same which was from the beginning, and he came before me, saying—Behold, here am I, send me, I will be thy son, and I will redeem all mankind, that one soul shall not be lost, and surely I will do it; wherefore give me thine honor. But, behold, my Beloved Son, which was my Beloved and Chosen from the beginning, said unto me—Father, thy will be done, and the glory be thine forever."*

*From these remarks made by the well beloved Son, we should naturally infer that in the discussion of the subject, the Father had made known His will and developed His plan and design pertaining to these matters. And all that His well beloved Son wanted to do was to carry out the will of His Father, as it would appear had been before expressed. He also wished the glory to be given to His Father, who as God the Father, and the originator and designer of the plan, had a right to all the honor and glory. But Lucifer wanted to introduce a plan contrary to the will of the Father, and then wanted His honor, and said 'I will redeem all mankind, that one soul shall not be lost, and surely I will do it; wherefore give me thine honor.'*

*He wanted to go contrary to the will of this Father and presumptuously sought to deprive man of his free agency, thus making him a serf, and placing him in a position in which it was impossible for him to obtain that exaltation which God designed should be man's, through obedience to the law which He had suggested; and again, Lucifer wanted the honor and power of his Father, to enable him to carry out principles which were contrary to the Father's wish"*

John Taylor – Mediation and Atonement. Pp.93, 94

From 1829 through 1844, the Prophet Joseph Smith learned much about the pre-earth life. As early as 1830, while working on the inspired translation of the Bible, it was revealed to him that *"all the children of men" were created "spiritually, before they were naturally upon the face of the earth."* (**Moses 3:5.**)

Some years later, while translating the Book of Abraham, he learned that Abraham saw in vision "the intelligences that were organized before the world was"— the spirits who stood in God's presence in that pre-earth existence. Abraham saw that there "were many of the noble and great ones" among those spirits." (**Abr. 3:22– 23.**)

Speaking of these things, Joseph Smith said,

> *"At the first organization in heaven, we were all present and saw the Savior chosen and appointed and the plan of salvation made, and we sanctioned it."* The Words of Joseph Smith (Provo: Religious Studies Center, Brigham Young University, 1980) p. 60

There were others, however, who were less noble. Many of the spirits, exercising their agency, chose to follow Lucifer in rebellion against God.

> "And it came to pass that Adam, being tempted of the devil—for, behold, the devil was before Adam, for he rebelled against me, saying, Give me thine honor, which is my power; and also a third part of the hosts of heaven turned he away from me because of their agency;" (**D&C 29:36**)

And the angels which kept not their first estate, but left their own habitation, he hath reserved in everlasting chains under darkness unto the judgment of the great day. (**Jude 1:6.**)

Lucifer, as the Lord revealed to Joseph Smith, was once;

> *"an angel of God who was in authority in the presence of God, who rebelled against the Only Begotten Son" and "sought to take the kingdom of our God and his Christ." (D&C 76:25, 28; see Isa.*

*14:12–15.) Lucifer's proposals that "one soul shall not be lost"*
*(tempting as it sounds, it would nevertheless suspend our agency to*
*choose) and that he be given God's place and glory were rejected.*
*(See Moses 4:1–3.) War followed, and because of his rebellion,*
*Lucifer "was thrust down from the presence of God and the Son,*
*and was called Perdition." (D&C 76:25– 26; see Rev. 12:7–9.)*

Some spirits who sanctioned our Heavenly Father's plan were foreordained to special callings on earth. Such spirits come to earth not predetermined but predisposed to recognize and obey the voice of truth. Not only were Abraham and Jeremiah called in this way (see Abr. 3:23; Jer. 1:5), but also, as Joseph Smith taught, *"every man who has a calling to minister to the inhabitants of the world was ordained to that very purpose in the grand Council of Heaven before this world was."* The Words of Joseph Smith (Provo: Religious Studies Center, Brigham Young University, 1980) p. 367. See also p. 371; Alma 13:1–5

I suppose that in that grand council I was ordained to serve the young men of the Garden Heights North Ward, as well as other callings I have been blessed to receive.

In addition to the scriptures and the references above, the following were very helpful in gathering the information for this section:

- "The Restoration of Major Doctrines through Joseph Smith: The Godhead, Mankind, and the Creation," Donald Q. Cannon, Larry E. Dahl, and John W. Welch, Ensign, Jan 1989

- "Mediation and Atonement" by John Taylor

- "Jesus the Christ" by James E. Talmage

# The Second Day of Christmas

*"We will make an earth whereon these may dwell."*

## Creation of the World

The war in Heaven had ended, and now we required a place—a world where we could exercise the agency we had fought to preserve. And who better to shape that world than our Captain, the One foreordained to be our Savior? It was Christ who was chosen to create the very earth where He Himself would one day walk, teach, and be crucified.

Of course, we understand that such a work was not accomplished in a single day. Yet, imagine the moment when He stood back, surveyed His creation, and declared, "It is good." What a day that must have been! A reward, perhaps, in its own way—the satisfaction of shaping a world so grand, so filled with life, so perfectly set in motion. Until man arrived.

For a time, everything was good. But then came agency, and with it, the inevitable consequences of choice. That, however, is a story for another day.

Abraham came to understand a profound truth: just as one planet or star surpasses another in glory until reaching Kolob—the great governing star **(Abr. 3:9)**—so too, among spirits, there is a hierarchy of greatness until all lead to the ultimate governing One—Jesus Christ **(Abr. 3:19, 24)**.

> "And there stood one among them that was like unto God, and he said unto those who were with him: We will go down, for there is space there, and we will take of these materials, and we will make an earth whereon these may dwell" **(Abr. 3:24)**.

Abraham's record stands as the earliest scriptural witness of this vital truth.

In this connection the Prophet Joseph Smith taught:

> *"You ask the learned doctors why they say the world was made out of nothing; and they will answer, 'Doesn't the Bible say He created*

*the world?' And they infer, from the word create, that it must
have been made out of nothing. Now, the word create came from
the [Hebrew] word baurau which does not mean to create out of
nothing; it means to organize; the same as a man would organize
materials and build a ship."(Teachings, 350; emphasis in original.)*

## Embracing Materiality: The Creation

Joseph Smith's teachings on the creation of the world went hand in hand with the doctrine of man's eternal nature. While many believed that God created the world ex nihilo—out of nothing—Joseph revealed a far different truth: God organized the earth from pre-existing matter. In defining creation as "organization," the Prophet provided profound insight into the nature of physical matter, the attributes of God, and the purpose of mortality itself.

To understand creation is to understand that God is a Being of order and law, not one who acts on whims. The universe is not chaos—it moves according to divine system and structure.

Joseph's understanding of creation deepened over time. From that pivotal moment in 1820, when he stood in the Sacred Grove and saw with his own eyes that "God created man in his own image" (Gen. 1:27; see JS—H 1:16–17), to the revelations that followed, his knowledge expanded, piece by piece, until the great Restoration truths stood in full light.

Man was quite literally created in the image of God. By 1830, Joseph Smith had already been shown the staggering scope of God's creations, as the Lord declared, "Worlds without number have I created" (Moses 1:33). That same year, Joseph received another revelation, one that unveiled a deeper truth—every creation took place twice: first spiritually, then physically (D&C 29:31–32; Moses 3:5).

At that time, Joseph understood with certainty that God the Father had created "this heaven, and this earth" through His Only Begotten Son, Jesus Christ (Moses 2:1; John 1:10–14). But his understanding of the Creation did not stop there. In 1835, while translating the book of Abraham, Joseph discovered even more about how the world came to be. He learned that Christ did not act alone but worked in concert with other divine beings in the process of creation: "Then the Lord said: Let us go down. And they went down at the beginning, and they, that is the Gods, organized and formed the heavens and the earth" (Abr. 4:1).

With each revelation, Joseph's knowledge of the Creation expanded, revealing a universe governed not by randomness, but by divine order, law, and purpose.

Whether this concept was an extrapolation or a distortion of earlier Christian beliefs about the Creation is impossible to say. What is clear, however, is that Joseph Smith was restoring a truth once known to Abraham but long since lost.

One of the great revelations Joseph uncovered was that the Creation was not an act of conjuring something from nothing, but rather a process of organization. During the Nauvoo period, he continued to emphasize this point. His private secretary, William Clayton, recorded in 1841 that the Prophet taught, "This earth was organized or formed out of other planets which were broke up and remodeled and made into the one on which we live" (Words, p. 60).

This was a radical departure from traditional Christian thought, yet it reinforced a vital truth: God is a Being of order, shaping and refining His creations according to eternal laws, rather than creating from nothing.

In his renowned King Follett discourse, delivered during the April 1844 general conference, Joseph Smith offered one of his most profound teachings on creation as organization. He explained to the Saints that the word create comes from the Hebrew bara, meaning to organize, not to make something from nothing. He declared that "God had materials to organize the world out of chaos ... [which] may be organized and reorganized but not destroyed" (Teachings, pp. 350–52).

This revelation reframed the very nature of creation. The universe was not an arbitrary act of divine will, but a process of order and purpose—one governed by eternal laws. For those seeking a deeper understanding of this sermon, the most comprehensive version can be found in The Prophet Joseph Smith's King Follett Discourse: A Six Column Comparison of Original Notes and Amalgamations by Donald Q. Cannon and Larry E. Dahl (Provo: BYU Religious Studies Center, 1983).

In that council in heaven our Heavenly Father announced His divine plan. 2 Ne. 9:13; Alma 34:9; Abr. 3:22–27 It is also called:

- the plan of happiness, Alma 42:8, 16.

- the plan of salvation, Jarom 1:2; Alma 24:14; Alma  42:5; Moses 6:62

- the plan of redemption, Jacob 6:8; Alma 12:25–34;  Alma 17:16; Alma 18:39; Alma 22:13; Alma 29:2;  Alma 34:16, 31; Alma 39:18; Alma 42:11–13

- the plan of restoration, Alma 41:2.

- the plan of mercy, Alma 42:15, 31; 2 Ne. 9:6.

- the plan of deliverance, 2 Ne. 11:5.

- and the everlasting gospel. Rev. 14:6; D&C 27:5;  D&C 36:5; D&C 68:1; D&C 77:8–9, 11; D&C 79:1; D&C 84:103; D&C 99:1; D&C 101:22, 39; D&C 106:2; D&C 109:29, 65; D&C 124:88; D&C 128:17; D&C 133:36; D&C 135:3, 7; D&C 138:19, 25; JS— H 1:34.  The purpose of the plan is to provide opportunity for the spirit children of God to progress toward an eternal exaltation.

- The plan required the Creation, and that in turn required both the Fall and the Atonement.

## These are the three fundamental components of the plan.

- The creation of a paradisiacal planet came from  God. Latter-day revelation affirms that Michael (known also as Adam; see D&C 27:11; D&C 107:54; D&C 128:21) participated in the process of creation as well.

- Mortality and death came into the world through the Fall of Adam. (2 Ne. 2:25; Moses 6:48; JST, Gen. 6:49)

- Immortality and the possibility of eternal life were provided by the Atonement of Jesus Christ. (2 Ne. 2:21–28)

- The Creation, the Fall, and the Atonement were planned long before the actual work of the Creation began.

## Phases of the Creation

The Creation was not a haphazard event but a carefully planned process, designed and ordered before it ever took physical form. As scripture declares, "the Lord God created all things … spiritually, before they were naturally upon the face of the earth" (Moses 3:5; see also Moses 6:51).

The physical Creation unfolded in a series of distinct, structured periods. In Genesis and the book of Moses, these phases are called days (Gen. 1:5–2:3; Moses 2:5–3:3). In the book of Abraham, they are referred to as times (Abr. 4:8–5:3). Whether described as days, times, or ages, each phase marked a division of eternity—one identifiable event leading into the next (Abr. 3:4).

- **Period One:** The atmospheric heavens and the physical earth took form. Light emerged from darkness, the first great act of organization. (Gen. 1:1–5; Moses 2:1–5; Abr. 4:1–5).

- **Period Two:** The waters were separated—some gathered upon the earth's surface, others forming the atmospheric heavens. This allowed for clouds and rain, ensuring life could one day flourish. (Gen. 1:6–8; Moses 2:6–8; Abr. 4:6–8).

- **Period Three:** The earth was prepared to bring forth life. Grasses, herbs, and trees appeared, each carrying its own seed, ensuring the continuation of its kind. (Gen. 1:9–13; Moses 2:9–13; Abr. 4:9–13).

- **Period Four:** Order extended beyond the earth. The sun, moon, and stars were placed in precise relationship, governing the flow of time, setting the seasons, and ensuring the rhythms of life. The sun, a vast furnace of hydrogen, was positioned to provide heat and light, sustaining all creation. (Gen. 1:14–19; Moses 2:14–19; Abr. 4:14–19).

• **Period Five:** Life in the waters and sky began. Fish and fowl were formed, each after its own kind, given the ability to multiply and fill the earth. (Gen. 1:20–23; Moses 2:20–23; Abr. 4:20–23).

• **Period Six:** The earth teemed with living creatures. Beasts, cattle, and every creeping thing were created, again, each after its kind. This was the culmination of earth's preparation—setting the stage for the crowning creation yet to come. (Gen. 1:24–31; Moses 2:24–31; Abr. 4:24–31).

The Creation was not an act of chaos but one of divine precision, an ordered unfolding of God's eternal plan.

## Then the Gods counseled together and declared:

> "Let us go down and form man in our image, after our likeness… So the Gods went down to organize man in their own image, in the image of the Gods to form they him, male and female to form they them." (Abr. 4:26–27)

Thus, Adam and Eve were formed. It's worth noting that the Lord called both the man and the woman "Adam" (Gen. 5:2; Moses 6:9), uniting them under a single name. And from the beginning, they were given a charge—one that echoes through every generation since:

> "Be fruitful, and multiply, and replenish the earth, and subdue it: and have dominion over the fish of the sea, and over the fowl of the air, and over every living thing that moveth upon the earth." (Gen. 1:28; Moses 2:28; see also Abr. 4:28; JST, Gen. 1:30)

With this, the grand work of Creation reached its conclusion, and the seventh period was designated as a time of rest. Henry Eyring noted, this moment signified a divine pause—a reflection upon all that had been brought into existence (World of Evidence, World of Faith, in Of Heaven and Earth: Reconciling Scientific Thought with LDS Theology, ed. David L. Clark, 1998, p. 59).

Yet, the Lord did not simply create the earth and leave it to its own devices. He entrusted it to us, declaring:

> "It is expedient that I, the Lord, should make every man accountable, as a steward over earthly blessings, which I have made and prepared for my creatures. I, the Lord, stretched out the heavens, and built the earth, my very handiwork; and all things therein are mine. And it is my purpose to provide for my

saints, for all things are mine." (D&C 104:13–15; see also Rev. 7:3)

That stewardship is not a casual responsibility. It is a sacred trust. The very earth upon which we walk, the air we breathe, and the life that fills this world—it is all the Lord's handiwork. And if it belongs to Him, then how we care for it should reflect our reverence for the Creator Himself.

Then the Gods counseled together and said:

"Let us go down and form man in our image, after our likeness...

"So the Gods went down to organize man in their own image, in the image of the Gods to form they him, male and female to form they them." Abr. 4:26–27.

Thus, Adam and Eve were formed. Note that the Lord called the first man and woman "Adam" (see Gen. 5:2; Moses 6:9). And they were blessed to "be fruitful, and multiply, and replenish the earth, and subdue it: and have dominion over the fish of the sea, and over the fowl of the air, and over every living thing that moveth upon the earth." (Gen. 1:28; Moses 2:28; see also Abr. 4:28; JST, Gen. 1:30)

Here is just an interesting thing that I found in my research from Elder Nelson. The Lord has entrusted us to care for the earth. He said:

"It is expedient that I, the Lord, should make every man accountable, as a steward over earthly blessings, which I have made and prepared for my creatures. I, the Lord, stretched out the heavens, and built the earth, my very handiwork; and all things therein are mine. And it is my purpose to provide for my saints, for all things are mine" (D&C 104:13–15; see also Rev. 7:3)

I think this means that we should be pretty conscientious of this blessing we call the earth.

In addition to the Scriptures these resources provided great insights on the Creation.

• Andrew Skinner, "The Book of Abraham: A Most  Remarkable Book," Ensign, Mar 1997,  Russell M. Nelson, "The Creation," Ensign, May 2000

• Donald Q. Cannon, Larry E. Dahl, and John W. Welch,  "The Restoration of Major Doctrines through Joseph Smith: The Godhead, Mankind, and the Creation," Ensign, Jan 1989.

• See Russell M. Nelson, "The Magnificence of Man," Ensign, Jan. 1988, 64–69; "We Are Children of God," Ensign, Nov. 1998, 85–87.

# The Third Day of Christmas



*"So he drove out the man"*

## Kicking Adam out of the Garden of Eden

The Fall of Adam stands as one of the most pivotal events in the history of the world. Nearly every faith tradition acknowledges its essential role in the grand plan of salvation. While much has been said about the Fall itself, that is not that defining moment is not the big day in this recounting of the twelve days of Christmas.

The defining moment—the big day—was when the Savior Himself sent Adam and Eve out of the Garden. They did the falling, but Christ did the sending. That was the deal of all deals. In Genesis 3:8-24, it is recorded simply as "drove out the man," but those words carry a weight that shaped the destiny of all humankind.

Some might argue whether the greater moment was when man was granted agency or when Adam and Eve were expelled from Eden. But here's the key truth: when the Savior sent them out, He was establishing a divine pattern—the law of consequences. It was not punishment for punishment's sake; it was justice in its purest form. And in that moment, Christ committed Himself to the ultimate act of selflessness. It was the last chance to dodge the bullet, per se.

Think of it this way—had Adam and Eve remained in the Garden, there would have been no need for a Redeemer. The Fall necessitated the Atonement. The moment they stepped beyond Eden's gates, the Savior's role was sealed—He would come, suffer, and redeem. That moment wasn't just about leaving paradise; it was about ensuring the plan of salvation would move forward. That is when our Savior committed to the ultimate sacrifice.

While visiting the British Museum in London, Russell M. Nelson came across a most unusual book. It wasn't scripture but an English translation of an ancient Egyptian manuscript. From its pages, he quoted a dialogue between the Father and the Son. Referring to His Father, Jehovah—the pre-mortal Christ—declared:

*"He took the clay from the hand of the angel, and made Adam according to Our image and likeness, and He left him lying for forty days and forty nights without putting breath into him. And He heaved sighs over him daily, saying, 'If I put breath into this [man], he must suffer many pains.' And I said unto My Father, 'Put breath into him; I will be an advocate for him.' And My Father said unto Me, 'If I put breath into him, My beloved Son, Thou wilt be obliged to go down into the world, and to suffer many pains for him before Thou shalt have redeemed him, and made him to come back to his primal state.' And I said unto My Father, 'Put breath into him; I will be his advocate, and I will go down into the world, and will fulfill Thy command.'"*

"Discourse on Abbatôn by Timothy, Archbishop of Alexandria," in Coptic Martyrdoms etc. in the Dialect of Upper Egypt, ed. and trans. E. A. Wallis Budge (1914), 482. Timothy, archbishop of Alexandria, died in a.d. 385. Brackets are included in Budge's English translation.

While this text is not scripture, it echoes scriptural truths—truths that reaffirm the deep, abiding love of the Father for the Son, and the Son's willing sacrifice for us. Christ was not compelled; He volunteered. "For God so loved the world, that he gave his only begotten Son" (John 3:16). He laid down His life willingly, not by force (John 10:14–15, 17–18).

From the very beginning, the Lord declared His purpose: "This is my work and my glory—to bring to pass the immortality and eternal life of man" (Moses 1:39). The breath of life, the gift of agency, and the law of consequences were all woven into the fabric of creation. So when the Lord "drove them out" of Eden, it was not a last-minute decision. It was the fulfillment of a divine plan, executed with absolute consistency. That kind of unwavering commitment is something I admire deeply—it sets a pattern I strive to follow.

## Let me put this into perspective with a real-life example.

A young couple, devoted to raising their children with love and discipline, faced a moment of truth when their son decided to test his hammering skills—on the dashboard of the family's Suburban. The entertainment system? Destroyed. The climate controls? Obliterated.

Now, what do you do? The boy was too young for a proper beating—that sort of thing is best reserved for the teenage years. He was also too young to ever pay for the damages. But doing nothing wasn't an option. The sacrifice of that poor dashboard had to mean something. A lesson had to be learned.

So, these parents devised a plan. Not a punishment meant to crush the child, but a process of restitution—something within his ability, yet demanding enough to teach respect, responsibility, and a bit of hard work. It required supervision. It required patience. And most of all, it required sacrifice—not from the child, but from the parents. They spent countless Saturdays guiding him through the consequences of his actions.

And the result? That boy grew into a respectful, capable young man.

Now, here's the point: the punishment cost the parents far more than it cost the child. If they had simply waived the need for restitution, they could have saved themselves time, effort, and a dozen weekends. But good parents don't take the easy way out.

When Christ drove Adam and Eve out of the Garden, He wasn't punishing them in anger—He was practicing perfect parenting. He enforced consequences, not because He wanted to, but because He had to. And just like those parents who sacrificed to teach their son, Christ sacrificed infinitely more to redeem us.

That is perfect love.

**Now, let's look at something fascinating about the Fall.**

The book of Abraham offers a unique insight—one not found elsewhere in scripture—regarding the physical location of the earth before the Fall.

Consider the time reference in this verse:

"But of the tree of knowledge of good and evil, thou shalt not eat of it; for in the time that thou eatest thereof, thou shalt surely die. Now I, Abraham, saw that it was after the Lord's time, which was after the time of Kolob; for as yet the Gods had not appointed unto Adam his reckoning" (Abr. 5:13).

Joseph Fielding Smith taught that Adam lived according to Kolob's time before his transgression (Doctrines of Salvation, 1:79). Brigham Young went further, explaining that before the Fall, the earth itself was near the very throne of God. When Adam and Eve fell, the planet quite literally moved—leaving the presence of God and assuming its current position in our solar system.

And here's where it gets really interesting—one day, when all the effects of the Fall are reversed, the earth will not just be redeemed spiritually. It will physically return to the presence of God.

That's not just restoration—it's a homecoming.

 Here are President Young's words:

> *"When the earth was framed and brought into existence and man was placed upon it, it was near the throne of our Father in heaven. ... But when man fell, the earth fell into space, and took up its*

(Journal of Discourses, 17:143.)

The power by which the effects of Adam's Fall are overcome for all created things, including the earth, is the Atonement of Jesus Christ (see D&C 76:40–43; Moses 7:48–62).

So He drove out the man – This was an ultimate – selfless – demonstration of perfect parenting. He taught, warned, encouraged, and enforced consequences, even when it required His own great sacrifice.

The fall of Adam is one of the most important occurrences in the history of man. Before the fall, Adam and Eve had physical bodies but no blood. There was no sin, no death, and no children among any of the earthly creations. With the eating of the "forbidden fruit," Adam and Eve became mortal, sin entered, blood formed in their bodies, and death became a part of life. Adam became the "first flesh" upon the earth (Moses 3: 7), meaning that he and Eve were the first to become mortal. After Adam fell, the whole creation fell and became mortal. Adam's fall brought both physical and spiritual death into the world upon all mankind. (Hel. 14: 16-17).

Because God knew that the Fall would occur, he had planned in the pre-mortal life for a Savior. Jesus Christ came in the meridian of time to atone for the fall of Adam and also for man's individual sins on condition of man's repentance.

# The Fourth Day of Christmas



*"Zion have I blessed, but the residue of the people have I cursed."*

**Enoch and Noah – the first real societal success
followed by a global failure.**

I'm going to take a little liberty here and call two events—separated by centuries—one day. Given that they happened thousands of years ago, I think we can get away with it. And considering the Lord's reckoning of time, I do it with a clear conscience.

On one hand, we have Enoch and the City of Zion—a people who lived in perfect harmony with God's commandments. They built a society so righteous, so unified, that the Lord took them up. It was textbook salvation—proof that when people fully embrace God's laws, unparalleled joy follows. A perfect success.

On the other hand, we have Noah and his family—people of the same spiritual caliber as those in Zion, but called to a vastly different mission. Instead of living in a world of righteousness, they were chosen to endure its total collapse. The people around them had sunk so deep into wickedness that the Spirit withdrew entirely, and the flood came.

Now, let's be clear—this wasn't a failure on the Lord's part. Man had his agency, and nearly all of humanity chose destruction. So, if we're talking about global outcomes, it was a catastrophic failure—not for God, but for mankind. Only eight souls survived.

Looking at these two events together, maybe I shouldn't use the words success and failure—perhaps blessed and cursed are more fitting. One group was exalted; the other was washed away. And though those two outcomes unfolded centuries apart, in the grand scheme of things, let's just say…

It all happened on the same day.

> "But the Lord said unto Enoch: Zion have I blessed, but the
> residue of the people have I cursed." So righteous were the people

of Enoch's city that "Zion, in process of time, was taken up into heaven." (Moses 7.)

"And Enoch walked with God: and he was not; for God took him." (Genesis 5: 24)

Today, we're often told that the world mirrors the days of Noah—that wickedness runs rampant, just as it did before the Flood. But I believe something else is true as well. The righteousness of Enoch's time also exists among us.

The difference? We don't have the luxury of gathering in one place, building a Zion, and separating ourselves from the world. That's not our calling. Instead, we are scattered—tasked with gathering the elect from every nation, tribe, and people. But make no mistake—just as in the days of Enoch and Noah, a separation will come. The elect will be taken, and the wicked will face destruction.

The records of these two towering prophets—Enoch and Noah—are found in Genesis 5 and 6, as well as in Moses 6 through 9. Their influence echoes throughout scripture, and countless writings have explored their lives, teachings, and legacies.

I've come across so many fascinating insights that I decided to include some of them here. No particular order, no rigid structure—just timeless truths, waiting to be read.

So, kick off your shoes… and let's dive in.

One important point I need to emphasize is a phrase found in 1 Peter, where he states:

> "For Christ also hath once suffered for sins, the just for the unjust, that he might bring us to God, being put to death in the flesh, but quickened by the Spirit: by which also he went and preached unto the spirits in prison; which sometime were disobedient, when once the longsuffering of God waited in the days of Noah, while the ark was a preparing, wherein few, that is, eight souls were saved by water.' (1 Pet. 3:18-20.)

As I read these verses, three key insights stood out to me:

- Christ suffered for both the people of Enoch's City—who had to repent and change to become a Zion society—and for Noah's neighbors, who refused to repent but were still promised the gospel in the spirit prison.

- Even those who were destroyed in the flood were not beyond Christ's mercy.

- Christ's long-suffering is a divine attribute I must develop if I hope to be part of the "Day 13" we'll discuss later.

I am deeply grateful for modern revelation, which gives us a fuller understanding of Enoch. Without it, this is all the Book of Genesis tells us about him:

> "And Jared lived after he begat Enoch eight hundred years, and begat sons and daughters:
>
> And all the days of Jared were nine hundred sixty and two years: and he died.
>
> And Enoch lived sixty and five years, and begat Methuselah:
>
> And Enoch walked with God after he begat Methuselah three hundred years, and begat sons and daughters:
>
> And all the days of Enoch were three hundred sixty and five years:
>
> And Enoch walked with God: and he was not; for God took him." (Genesis 5:19 – 24)

Back in high school, I picked up Neal A. Maxwell's book Of One Heart. It wasn't too long, so I gave it a read. In it, he explored the City of Enoch, what it takes to be translated, and, most importantly, what a Zion society really looks like. I found it fascinating, so I've included some key excerpts here.

> *First, in a world where nations are in turmoil and despair is everywhere, it's crucial to remember that thousands of years ago, an entire people successfully lived God's commandments—and in doing so, they found unparalleled happiness.*
>
> *Second, the Lord provides both incentives and warnings. It's just as important to study the blessings of righteousness as it is to understand the consequences of sin.*
>
> *Third, despite the overwhelming evil that surrounded them, God preserved and prepared Enoch's people. And He has promised that in our time, though "great tribulations shall be among the children of men,… my people will I preserve" (Moses 7:6). The Lord also declared that there will come a day when peace will be taken from the earth and the adversary will hold power over his dominion. But—just as surely—"the Lord shall have power over his saints, and shall reign in their midst" (D&C 1:35-36).*
>
> *Fourth, the prophesied reunion of Enoch's people with the righteous on earth at the time of Christ's Second Coming will be unlike*

*anything in human history. It's worth some quiet anticipation.*

*Now, consider how this all began—Enoch, standing alone, except for his heavenly helpers. Then a small band joined him. A colony. A city. And finally, a Zion society.*

There was no new or complex doctrine that made this possible. You won't find a single revolutionary teaching that led to the translation of Enoch's city. What set these people apart was their steady, consistent application of the simple teachings of Jesus Christ. That's the heart of the message Elder Maxwell emphasized.

*Since Enoch's people were worthy of translation, Elder Maxwell assumes they were at least as righteous as the Nephites during the golden era of Fourth Nephi (A.D. 36–111). So, I've included some of their defining characteristics here.*

On the other hand, the rest of the world in Enoch's time was described as the most wicked of all God's creations. Elder Maxwell suggests they were at least as corrupt as the Nephites in A.D. 400–421 (see Moroni 9). So, for contrast, I've included those descriptions at the end of this section.

Here is Elder Maxwell's Synopsis of the City and People of Enoch

*Enoch's father, Jared, "taught Enoch in all the ways of God." Enoch was 25 years old when he was ordained under the hand of Adam, and he was 65 when Adam blessed him—the same year Enoch begat Methuselah. Enoch walked with God 365 years, and he was 430 years old when he was translated.*

*When he was about 65 years of age, Enoch journeyed among men, and the Spirit of God descended out of heaven and abode upon him. A voice from heaven told him to prophesy and call others to repentance, for the Lord was angry with the people, saying that "their hearts have waxed hard, and their ears are dull of hearing, and their eyes cannot see afar off." The people had gone astray, had denied the Lord, had foresworn themselves by their oaths, had sought their own counsel in the dark, had devised murder, and had not kept commandments.*

*Enoch humbly asked why he had found favor, for he described himself as "but a lad," as "slow of speech," and "all the people hate me." The Lord told him to go and do as commanded, and "no man shall pierce thee." He was told to "open thy mouth and it shall be filled." He was told to say to his people, "Choose ye this day to serve the Lord God." He was promised that mountains would flee before him and rivers would turn from their courses.*

*A saying subsequently went abroad in the land: "A seer hath the Lord raised up unto his people." In his testifying and prophesying Enoch was regarded by many as "a strange thing" and "a wild man," and at first "all men were offended because of him."*

*As he journeyed from the land of Cainan, by the sea east, he had a vision. Subsequently he preached and unfolded the plan of salvation, and the people "trembled, and could not stand in his presence. In recounting a vision on Mount Simeon, he taught the doctrine of the Fall and Atonement.*

*Enoch showed great faith and later led the people of God against their enemies. Mountains fled and rivers were actually diverted at his command. Over many years he continued to preach righteousness and built a city—the "City of Holiness—even Zion," and the Lord called this people Zion. Other nations feared Zion greatly, and there were wars and bloodshed among the residue, for "they are without affection, and they hate their own blood."*

*But Enoch's people came to be of one heart, one mind; they dwelt in righteousness and there were no poor among them, and the glory of the Lord was upon His people. Zion, in process of time (365 years), was taken up into God's own bosom. The saying then went forth, "Zion is fled."*

Here are several Quotations from Church Leaders about Enoch

**SPENCER W. KIMBALL** *"Again, we thank thee, O God, for another prophet who helped to set the lines straight for us—Enoch... ..(Conference Report, April 1974, p. 66.)*

**JOSEPH SMITH** *"And now, I ask, how righteousness and truth are going to sweep the earth as with a flood? I will answer. Men and angels are to be coworkers in bringing to pass this great work, and Zion is to be prepared, even a new Jerusalem, for the elect that are to be gathered from the four quarters of the earth, and to be established an holy city... ... (History of the Church, 2:260.)*

**JOSEPH FIELDING SMITH** *"The people of the city of Enoch, because of their integrity and faithfulness, were as pilgrims and strangers on the earth. This is due to the fact that they were living the celestial law in a telestial world, and all were of one mind, perfectly obedient to all commandments of the Lord." (Church History and Modern Revelation, 1953, 1:195.)*

*"In the day of regeneration, when all things are made new, there will be three great cities that will be holy. One will be the Jerusalem of old which shall be rebuilt according to the prophecy of Ezekiel. One will be the city of Zion, or of Enoch, which was taken from*

*the earth when Enoch was translated and which will be restored;
and the city Zion, or New Jerusalem, which is to be built by the
seed of Joseph on this the American continent." (Answers to Gospel
Questions, Deseret Book Co., 1958, 2:105.)*

Of that day President Joseph Fielding Smith wrote:

*"Enoch saw in vision the kingdoms of the world and all their
inhabitants down even to the end of time. The Lord told him of
Noah and the flood and how he would destroy the people of the
earth for their iniquity. Of these rebellious ones who rejected the
truth and paid no heed to the preachings of Noah and the ancient
prophets, the Lord said: `I can stretch forth mine hands and hold
all the creations which I have made; and mine eye can pierce them
also, and among all the workmanship of mine hands there has not
been so great wickedness as among thy brethren.*

*"`But behold, their sins shall be upon the heads of their fathers;
Satan shall be their father, and misery shall be their doom, and the
whole heavens shall weep over them, even all the workmanship of
mine hands; wherefore should not the heavens weep, seeing these
shall suffer? But behold, these which thine eyes are upon shall
perish in the floods; and behold, I will shut them up; a prison have I
prepared for them. And That which I have chosen hath plead before
my face. Wherefore, he suffereth for their sins; inasmuch as they
will repent in the day that my Chosen shall return unto me, and
until that day they shall be in torment. (Moses 7:36-39.)'"*

President Smith then says:

*"From this we learn that the Lord has prepared a prison for the
souls of all those who rejected the testimony of the antediluvian
prophets, where they were to remain in torment until the time when
Jesus should atone for their sins and return to the Father."*

(Bruce R. McConkie, comp., Doctrines of Salvation 2<br>
[Bookcraft, 1955]: 156-57. Italics in original.)

It is interesting that the city of Enoch will return to the earth. Of this
President Smith has said:

*"In the day of regeneration, when all things are made new, there
will be three great cities that will be holy. One will be the Jerusalem
of old which shall be rebuilt according to the prophecy of Ezekiel.
One will be the city of Zion, or of Enoch, which was taken from the
earth when Enoch was translated and which will be restored; and
the city Zion, or New Jerusalem, which is to be built by the seed of
Joseph on this the American continent."*

34

Then President Smith quotes this scripture:

*"And righteousness will I send down out of heaven; and truth
will I send forth out of the earth, to bear testimony of mine
Only Begotten; his resurrection from the dead; yea, and also the
resurrection of all men; and righteousness and truth will I cause to
sweep the earth as with a flood, to gather out mine elect from the
four quarters of the earth, unto a place which I shall prepare, an
Holy City, that my people may gird up their loins, and be looking
forth for the time of my coming; for there shall be my tabernacle,
and it shall be called Zion, a New Jerusalem.*

*"And the Lord said unto Enoch: Then shalt thou and all thy city
meet them there, and we will receive them into our bosom, and
they shall see us; and we will fall upon their necks, and they shall
fall upon our necks, and we will kiss each other;*

*"And there shall be mine abode, and it shall be Zion, which shall
come forth out of all the creations which I have made; and for the
space of a thousand years the earth shall rest. (Moses 7:62-64.)"*

(Joseph Fielding Smith, Jr., comp., Answers to Gospel<br>Questions 2 [Deseret Book, 1958]: 105-6.)

**JOHN TAYLOR** *"Thus the people in that day, had had fair
warning, but only a very few paid any attention to it." (Journal of
Discourses, 24:291.)*

*"But we learn that there was a Church organized about as ours
may be; we learn that they went forth and preached the Gospel...
Enoch preached the Gospel to the people, and so did hundreds
of Elders as they are doing today; and they gathered the people
together and built up a Zion to the Lord... ..(JD, 26:34.)*

*"And as they gathered out from among the people, the Spirit of
God was withdrawn from among the people; and they became
exceedingly angry, angry at Enoch and angry at those who preached
the Gospel to them." (JD, 26:89-90.)*

**WILFORD WOODRUFF** *"There were not men enough in the
days of Enoch who were willing to sustain that which was right; one
part or other had to leave the earth; and the Lord translated Enoch
and his city and took them home to Himself." (JD, 11:243.)*

**BRIGHAM YOUNG** *"How long did it take Enoch to purify his
people—to become holy and prepared for what we want this people to
be prepared for in a very few years? It took him 365 years." (JD, 4:269.)*

*"They had not a diversity of languages, but all spoke one language; they were not trained in the various traditions in which we have been, for they received only one from Adam; they were as intimately associated as we would be living in this City two hundred years."* (JD, 3:320.)

**BRUCE R. McCONKIE** *"When the perfect Zion—composed solely of the pure in heart (D.& C. 97:21)—is again established on earth, then the presence of the Lord will be felt there as his presence was found in the ancient city of that name. (Moses 7:16-19, 62-64.)"* (Mormon Doctrine, Bookcraft, 1966, p. 361.)

*"But during the nearly 700 years from the translation of Enoch to the flood of Noah, it would appear that nearly all of the faithful members of the Church were translated, for 'the Holy Ghost fell on many, and they were caught up by the powers of heaven into Zion.' (Moses 7:27.)"* (Ibid., p. 804.)

**FRANKLIN D. RICHARDS** *"We are trying to understand the Gospel as Enoch understood it and as Christ understood it, and to do business as they did it, living in co-operation and managing our affairs in the same way, but many of us are not willing to be taught in temporal matters."* (CA, April 1898, p. 18.)

**JOHN A. WIDTSOE** *"He (God] gave Enoch a system, known now as the Order of Enoch, or the United Order. It provided that all the citizens of Zion should work together, and that whatever was produced should be given into the Lord's storehouse, and that every man should be given from the common store according to his wants and needs... The people, taught by Enoch, were able to overcome the lower feelings , and to divide all things with each other, so that all were equal."* (Juvenile Instructor, 36 [1901] 364.)

*"Then it was that a light was lost on the earth; and a chill crept over its surface. The sons of men moved anxiously about and peeped hither and thither. In quiet voices, such as we use when a great leader in Israel has left us, they asked, 'Where is Enoch; where is Zion, the City of Holiness?' They answered, 'Zion is fled.' "* (Ibid., p. 366.)

As Elder Maxwell compared the city of Enoch to the people of Nephi following the appearance of the Lord following His resurrection, here is his synopsis of the People of Nephi

The Rise (A. D. 36 to A. D. 111—about 75 years)

The Church of Christ thrived, and every soul was converted. Cities expanded, populations grew, and prosperity followed. The people fasted, prayed, and gathered often to hear the word of the Lord. They lived the commandments they had received, and because of their faithfulness, miracles were abundant.

This society in this period of time is described as having:

- No contentions.
- No disputations.
- Every man dealing justly one with another.
- All things in common.
- No rich, poor, bond, or free.
- Peace and prosperity in the land.
- A love of God in the hearts of the people.
- No envyings, strifes, tumults, whoredoms, lyings, murders, or lasciviousness.
- No robbers, murderers, or any "-ites." "They were in one," "and surely there could not be a happier people."

The Decline (A.D. 111 to A.D. 245, about 134 years.) There was a general peace, but then a small group revolted from the church, and there began to be "Lamanites" again. The population increased, and there was exceeding prosperity. Other churches were built up and began to deny much of Christ's gospel. False prophets arose, other "-ites" (factions) appeared, and the Lamanites were once again taught to hate children of God.

Society toward the end of this period deteriorated and is described as having—

- Pride, such as in wearing costly apparel.
- Goods and substance no more in common.
- Classes and divisions among the people.
- Religious persecution.
- All manner of iniquity.
- Ostentatious church buildings. "And the more wicked part of the people did wax strong and became exceedingly more numerous than were the people of God."

It is interesting to compare the rise and fall of the people of Nephi to the city of Enoch and the remaining people destroyed by the flood. The results were the same. Exaltation and/or Destruction.

## So now let's focus on Noah and the flood (between 600 - 700 years later)

Elder Mark E. Peterson in his book "Noah and The Flood" talks about

Enoch and his mission.

> *"Leading directly to the flood and the work of Noah was the mission of Enoch, also one of the truly great ones, who was sent to earth for a specific purpose. In his day there was a great division among the people. The righteous apparently lived in a land called Canaan, where Enoch was raised. His fathers were "preachers of righteousness, and spake and prophesied, and called upon all men, everywhere, to repent; and faith was taught unto the children of men."*

> *"The fear of the Lord was upon all nations, so great was the glory of the Lord, which was upon his people. And the Lord blessed the land, and they were blessed upon the mountains, and upon the high places, and did flourish."  Now comes the first mention of the city of Zion, or the city of Enoch: "And the Lord called his people Zion, because they were of one heart and one mind, and dwelt in righteousness; and there was no poor among them."*

> *Enoch continued his preaching amid great miracles. "And it came to pass in his days, that he built a city that was called the City of Holiness, even Zion. And it came to pass that Enoch talked with the Lord; and he said unto the Lord: Surely Zion shall dwell in safety forever. But the Lord said unto Enoch: Zion have I blessed, but the residue of the people have I cursed."*

So righteous were the people of Enoch's city that "Zion, in process of time, was taken up into heaven." (Moses 7.)

Thus there came a separation between the righteous and the wicked. But the Lord left some of His leaders on the earth looking toward the time of the flood. He would continue to appeal to the rebellious to the very last, for He would leave them no excuse.

Elder Peterson continues; Noah was among the Great Prophets

Noah, who built the ark, was one of God's greatest servants, chosen before he was born as were others of the prophets. He was no eccentric, as many have supposed. Neither was he a mythical figure created only in legend. Noah was real. The flood was real. And so was the ark, as were the various species of life saved in the ark. It was all factual, fully documented in scripture, and was the doing of the Almighty.

Let no one downgrade the life and mission of this great prophet. Noah was so near perfect in his day that he literally walked and talked with God.

This telestial planet of ours was destined to pass through three great crises. Two were related to the Savior: one to his second coming, the other to the time when the earth will be celestialized. But the third— which was first in order of events—was the flood in which Noah was the central figure. His choice for this strategic position is itself a measure of the greatness of this man and of the confidence placed in him by the Almighty.

Noah cried repentance to a wicked world, warning all men that they must change their ways or die in a deluge. They paid no heed. The prophecy was fulfilled, the ark was built, the flood came, and the earth was cleansed of its filth. After the waters receded, the world was made ready for a new generation of human beings to be propagated through Noah and his sons.

Few men in any age were as great as Noah. In many respects he was like Adam, the first man. Both had served as ministering angels in the presence of God even after their mortal experience. Adam was Michael, the archangel, but Noah was Gabriel, one of those nearest to God. Of all the hosts of heaven, he was chosen to open the Christian era by announcing to Mary that she would become the mother of the Savior, Jesus Christ. He even designated the name by which the Redeemer should be known here on earth, saying He would be the Son of God.

The Prophet Joseph Smith properly identified Adam as Michael and Noah as Gabriel. It was revealed to him that Adam stands next to the Savior in the priesthood line, and that Noah stands next to Adam, placing him in third position from the Lord. (History of the Church 3:386.)

The Savior had been appointed as our Redeemer in the primeval council in heaven. (See Moses 4:1-4; Abr. 3:27-28.) He, too, must be born here to accomplish His great atonement.

Thus Gabriel was chosen to become Noah, a preacher of righteousness, the builder of the ark, the progenitor of the new beginning of mankind.

Elder Peterson speaks of Gabriel's ministry—a figure of great significance in both the Old and New Testaments. To the ancient prophets, Gabriel was no mere legend; he was a divine messenger who visited them personally. His role in the greatest event in human history—the mission of Jesus Christ—was unmistakable.

Gabriel ushered in the Christian era, announcing the birth of the Savior of the world. He also foretold the coming of John the Baptist, the one who would prepare the way for the Lord. Long before these events, he appeared to the prophet Daniel, revealing the coming of the Messiah and prophesying of Jerusalem's future. He even played a role in interpreting Belshazzar's vision. (Dan. 8:16-27; 9:16)

Gabriel's ministry was not just one of announcements—it was a direct and powerful testimony of the divine plan of salvation, unfolding through the ages.

Gabriel's announcement of the forthcoming birth of the Lord occurred in this way:

> "And in the sixth month the angel Gabriel was sent from God unto a city of Galilee, named Nazareth, to a virgin espoused to a man whose name was Joseph, of the house of David; and the virgin's name was Mary.

> "And the angel came in unto her, and said, Hail, thou that art highly favoured, the Lord is with thee: blessed art thou among women.

> "And when she saw him, she was troubled at his saying, and cast in her mind what manner of salutation this should be.

> "And the angel said unto her, Fear not, Mary: for thou hast found favour with God. And, behold, thou shalt conceive in thy womb, and bring forth a son, and shalt call his name JESUS. He shall be great, and shall be called the Son of the Highest: and the Lord God shall give unto him the throne of his father David: and he shall reign over the house of Jacob for ever; and of his kingdom there shall be no end.

> "Then said Mary unto the angel, How shall this be, seeing I know not a man?

> "And the angel answered and said unto her, The Holy Ghost shall come upon thee, and the power of the Highest shall overshadow thee: therefore also that holy thing which shall be born of thee shall be called the Son of God.

> "And, behold, thy cousin Elisabeth, she hath also conceived a son in her old age: and this is the sixth month with her, who was called barren. For with God nothing shall be impossible." (**Luke 1:26-37.**)

Apparently the same angel appeared to Joseph, Mary's espoused husband, for Matthew says:

> "Now the birth of Jesus Christ was on this wise: When as his mother Mary was espoused to Joseph, before they came together, she was found with child of the Holy Ghost. Then Joseph her husband, being a just man, and not willing to make her a publick example, was minded to put her away privily.

> "But while he thought on these things, behold, the angel of the Lord appeared unto him in a dream, saying, Joseph, thou son of David, fear not to take unto thee Mary thy wife: for that which is

conceived in her is of the Holy Ghost. And she shall bring forth
a son, and thou shalt call his name JESUS: for he shall save his
people from their sins." (**Matt. 1:18-21**)

An angel—likely Gabriel once again—appeared to Joseph, the husband of
Mary, after the birth of Jesus Christ. His message was urgent: take the child
and flee. Herod, in his ruthless ambition, sought to destroy the newborn King.
The scripture records:

> "And when they were departed, behold, the angel of the Lord
> appeareth to Joseph in a dream, saying, Arise, and take the young
> child and his mother, and flee into Egypt, and be thou there until
> I bring thee word: for Herod will seek the young child to destroy
> him." (Matt. 2:13)

> Time passed, and Herod's reign of terror came to an end. Once
> again, the angel returned to Joseph with another command: it
> was time to go home.

> "But when Herod was dead, behold, an angel of the Lord
> appeareth in a dream to Joseph in Egypt, saying, Arise, and take
> the young child and his mother, and go into the land of Israel: for
> they are dead which sought the young child's life. And he arose,
> and took the young child and his mother, and came into the land
> of Israel." (**Matt. 2:19-21**)

There's something remarkable about these angelic visitations. The messages
were directed to Joseph—the head of the household—though he was not the
biological father of Jesus. Heaven still recognized his sacred role as protector
and guide.

Now, turning to John the Baptist, we find yet another account of Gabriel's
ministry…

> "And there appeared unto him an angel of the Lord standing on
> the right side of the altar of incense. And when Zacharias saw
> him, he was troubled, and fear fell upon him.

> "But the angel said unto him, Fear not, Zacharias: for thy prayer
> is heard; and thy wife Elisabeth shall bear thee a son, and thou
> shalt call his name John. And thou shalt have joy and gladness;
> and many shall rejoice at his birth. For he shall be great in the
> sight of the Lord, and shall drink neither wine nor strong drink;
> and he shall be filled with the Holy Ghost, even from his mother's
> womb. And many of the children of Israel shall he turn to the
> Lord their God. And he shall go before him in the spirit and
> power of Elias, to turn the hearts of the fathers to the children,

and the disobedient to the wisdom of the just; to make ready a
people prepared for the Lord.

"And Zacharias said unto the angel, Whereby shall I know this?
for I am an old man, and my wife well stricken in years.

"And the angel answering said unto him, I am Gabriel, that stand
in the presence of God: and am sent to speak unto thee, and to
shew thee these glad tidings. And, behold, thou shalt be dumb,
and not able to speak, until the day that these things shall be
performed, because thou believest not my words, which shall be
fulfilled in their season." (**Luke 1:11-20.**)

## Noah: A Child of Promise

Noah's arrival was no accident—his birth was foretold and his destiny
secured by covenant long before he ever walked the earth. The Lord made a
promise to Enoch that through his lineage, Noah would come. Methuselah,
Enoch's son, also prophesied of Noah's birth and took great pride in the
fact that all future generations of mankind would descend from him. The
scripture records:

"And all the days of Enoch were four hundred and thirty years.
And it came to pass that Methuselah, the son of Enoch, was not
taken, that the covenants of the Lord might be fulfilled, which
he made to Enoch; for he truly covenanted with Enoch that
Noah should be of the fruit of his loins. And it came to pass that
Methuselah prophesied that from his loins should spring all the
kingdoms of the earth (through Noah), and he took glory unto
himself." (**Moses 8:1-3**)

The scriptures are silent on the details of Noah's marriage, but they do
record that he was 450 years old when Japheth was born. Forty-two years
later, Shem followed, and when Noah reached 500, Ham was born. Whether
there were other children before these three, we do not know.

What we do know is that Noah and his sons hearkened to the Lord. They
were called the sons of God, a title that spoke of their faithfulness. But not all
of their family remained righteous. The scriptures make a painful note that
the daughters of Noah's sons turned away, selling themselves to wickedness.

Ham, often cast as the wayward one in later interpretations, was actually
faithful. He, along with his father and brothers, walked with God. When
the time came for the flood, only Noah, his three sons, and their wives were
found worthy to enter the ark. No mention is made of children boarding
with them. The implication is stark—none of their posterity outside that
immediate circle were worthy of salvation.

## Enoch and Noah: A Tale of Two Missions

The contrast between Enoch and Noah is striking. Both were called of God, both labored in a world of wickedness, but the outcomes of their missions could not have been more different.

Enoch was given power as great as any prophet before or since. He commanded mountains, raised new land from the depths of the sea, and rebuked giants who sought to destroy his people. His enemies fell before him, and through his tireless preaching, an entire city embraced righteousness so fully that the Lord took it into heaven.

Noah's mission was not to build a city for translation but to prepare for destruction. The days of miracles to persuade the people had passed. Their hearts were so hardened that even the most wondrous signs would not have turned them from their wickedness. No record is given of Noah parting seas or calling fire from heaven. Instead, he and his sons preached the word, offering one final opportunity for repentance. But their primary work was to build an ark, to prepare for the flood, and to ensure that the human family would have a future.

Yet, Noah was no lesser man. The scriptures call him "a just man and perfect in his generation." He held the holy priesthood after the order of the Son of God and "walked with God, as did also his three sons, Shem, Ham, and Japheth." (**Moses 8:20-27**)

That phrase—walked with God—is significant. Noah's sons were not merely righteous by association. They, too, stood apart from the corruption of their time. They were called "the sons of God," and they bore that title with faithfulness.

Modern prophets and apostles have spoken much about Noah and his role in the great plan. Here are some of their insights.

> **PRESIDENT BRIGHAM YOUNG:** *"It [the earth] has already had a baptism. You who have read the Bible must know that that is Bible doctrine. What does it matter if it is not in the same words that I use, it is none the less true that it was baptized for the remission of sins. The Lord said, `I will deluge (or immerse) the earth in water for the remission of the sins of the people'; or if you will allow me to express myself in a familiar style, to kill all the vermin that were nitting, and breeding, and polluting its body; it was cleansed of its filthiness; and soaked in the water, as long as some of our people ought to soak. The Lord baptized the earth for the remission of sins, and it has been once cleansed for the filthiness that has gone out of it, which was in the inhabitants who dwelt upon its face." (Journal of Discourses 1:274.)*

*"Brethren and sisters, I wish you to continue in your ways of well doing; I desire that your minds may be opened more and more to see and understand things as they are. This earth, in its present condition and situation, is not a fit habitation for the sanctified; but it abides the law of its creation, has been baptized with water, will be baptized by fire and the Holy Ghost, and by-and-by will be prepared for the faithful to dwell upon." (JD 8:83.)*

**ELDER ORSON PRATT:** *"Another great change happened nearly two thousand years after the earth was made. It was baptized by water. A great flow of water came, the great deep was broken up, the windows of heaven were opened from on high, and the waters prevailed upon the face of the earth, sweeping away all wickedness and transgression—a similitude of baptism for the remission of sins. God requires the children of men to be baptized. What for? For the remission of sins. So he required our globe to be baptized by a flow of water, and all of its sins were washed away, not one sin remaining." (JD 21:323.)*

*"Both man and the earth are redeemed from the original sin without ordinances; but soon we find new sins committed by the fallen sons of Adam, and the earth became corrupted before the Lord by their transgressions. It needs redeeming ordinances for these second transgressions. The Lord ordained baptism, or immersion of the earth in water, as a justifying ordinance." (JD 1:291.)*

**PRESIDENT JOHN TAYLOR:** *"The earth, as a part of the creation of God, has fulfilled and will fulfill the measure of its creation. It has been baptized by water, it will be baptized by fire; it will be purified and become celestial, and be a fit place for celestial bodies to inhabit." (Times and Seasons 5:408-9.)*

Elder Peterson included this information about the earth.

The flood of Noah's time was strictly God's affair. He arranged it, he turned loose the waters upon the earth, and when the time came, he recalled the waters so that the land was dry in an incredibly short time.

Why baptize the earth?

The earth is a living thing. Is there not great significance in the scriptural references to the earth? While Enoch and the Lord discussed the wickedness of men,

"...it came to pass that Enoch looked upon the earth; and he heard a voice from the bowels thereof, saying: Wo, wo is me, the mother of men; I am pained, I am weary, because of the wickedness of my

children. When shall I rest, and be cleansed from the filthiness
which is gone forth out of me? When will my Creator sanctify
me, that I may rest, and righteousness for a season abide upon my
face?

"And when Enoch heard the earth mourn, he wept, and cried
unto the Lord, saying: O Lord, wilt thou not have compassion
upon the earth? Wilt thou not bless the children of Noah?

"And it came to pass that Enoch continued his cry unto the Lord,
saying: I ask thee, O Lord, in the name of thine Only Begotten,
even Jesus Christ, that thou wilt have mercy upon Noah and his
seed, that the earth might never more be covered by the floods."
(**Moses 7:48-50.**)

Note these words coming out of the bowels of the earth: "When will my
Creator sanctify me that I may rest and righteousness for a season abide upon
my face?" Is that allegory? Would God deal in allegory in circumstances like
these? Was not the voice real?

Should not the earth—a living thing—be similarly sanctified? It was
baptized with water in the flood. Eventually it will be baptized with fire,
thus becoming cleansed and sanctified, to be made into a celestial sphere as
the eternal home for the righteous. The Lord has told us: "The place where
God resides is a great Urim and Thummim. This earth, in its sanctified
and immortal state, will be made like unto crystal and will be a Urim
and Thummim to the inhabitants who dwell thereon, whereby all things
pertaining to an inferior kingdom, or all kingdoms of a lower order, will
be manifest to those who dwell on it; and this earth will be Christ's." (**D&C
130:8-9.**)

When the Lord gave the revelation found in D&C 88 of the Doctrine and
Covenants, He made this further explanation:

"And again, verily I say unto you, the earth abideth the law of a
celestial kingdom, for it filleth the measure of its creation, and
transgreseth not the law—wherefore, it shall be sanctified; yea,
notwithstanding it shall die, it shall be quickened again, and shall
abide the power by which it is quickened, and the righteous shall
inherit it." (**D&C 88:25-26.**)

The Lord was pleased with the sacrifice. Noah said,

"I will call on the name of the Lord, that he will not again curse
the ground any more for man's sake, for the imagination of man's
heart is evil from his youth; and that he will not again smite
any more every thing living, as he hath done, while the earth

remaineth; and, that seed-time and harvest, and cold and heat,
and summer and winter, and day and night, may not cease with
man.

"And God blessed Noah and his sons, and said unto them, Be
fruitful and multiply, and replenish the earth. And the fear of
you, and the dread of you shall be upon every beast of the earth,
and upon every fowl of the air, upon all that moveth upon the
earth, and upon all the fishes of the sea; into your hands are they
delivered." **(JST, Gen. 9:6-8.)**

The Lord answered Noah's prayers. He made a covenant with him that
there would be no more floods, and there would always be seed time and
harvest. Then He gave him the rainbow in the sky as the sign of the covenant.

"And God spake unto Noah, and to his sons with him, saying,
And I, behold, I will establish my covenant with you, which I
made upon your father Enoch, concerning your seed after you.

"And it shall come to pass, that every living creature that is with
you, of the fowl, and of the cattle, and of the beast of the earth
that is with you, which shall go out of the ark, shall not altogether
perish; neither shall all flesh be cut off any more by the waters of
the flood; neither shall there any more be a flood to destroy the
earth. And I will establish my covenant with you, which I made
unto Enoch, concerning the remnants of your posterity.

"And God made a covenant with Noah, and said, This shall be
the token of the covenant I make between me and you, and for
every living creature with you, for perpetual generations; I will
set my bow in the cloud; and it shall be for a token of a covenant
between me and the earth.

"And it shall come to pass, when I bring a cloud over the earth,
that the bow shall be seen in the cloud; and I will remember my
covenant, which I have made between me and you, for every
living creature of all flesh. And the waters shall no more become a
flood to destroy all flesh.

"And the bow shall be in the cloud; and I will look upon it,
that I may remember the everlasting covenant, which I made
unto thy father Enoch; that, when men should keep all my
commandments, Zion should again come on the earth, the city of
Enoch which I have caught up unto myself.

"And this is mine everlasting covenant, that when thy posterity
shall embrace the truth, and look upward, then shall Zion look

downward, and all the heavens shall shake with gladness, and
the earth shall tremble with joy; and the general assembly of
the church of the firstborn shall come down out of heaven, and
possess the earth, and shall have place until the end come. And
this is mine everlasting covenant, which I made with thy father
Enoch. And the bow shall be in the cloud, and I will establish my
covenant unto thee, which I have made between me and thee, for
every living creature of all flesh that shall be upon the earth.

"And God said unto Noah, This is the token of the covenant
which I have established between me and thee; for all flesh that
shall be upon the earth." **(JST, Gen. 9:15-25.)**

What can I say? Enoch and Noah were each called for their time, their
mission crafted by the hand of God for a purpose beyond human measure.
Both were mighty in the Lord, and both bore the weight of their calling with
unwavering faith. When I look at other great men—whether in scripture or
in my own life—I see the same pattern. The tasks they are given differ, their
outcomes appear unequal, yet who am I to judge? Success in God's work isn't
measured by numbers or by human reasoning. I've learned to set aside my
own notions of achievement and simply stand in awe of the remarkable souls
I have the privilege to know.

# THE FIFTH DAY OF CHRISTMAS

*"But thou shalt not sin any more."*

## Personal visit to the Brother of Jared

As I consider big days in my life, along with meaningful events, many of them relate to "Firsts" such as the first time I drove a car alone, the first time I kissed a girl, the first time I went to the temple (those two were not the same day), The first time I stood at a pulpit, knees shaking, delivering a talk in Primary. The first time I flew an airplane by myself, etc. Therefore as I consider all the big things in the Savior's life I figured He likely cherished a few "firsts."

One, in particular, stands out: the first time He revealed Himself to man. His own words, spoken to the Brother of Jared, leave no room for doubt:

> "Never have I showed myself unto man whom I have created, for never has man believed in me as thou hast." **(Ether 3:15)**

Now, if that statement causes you to pause—if something in the back of your mind whispers, "But wait… what about Adam and Eve? What about Enoch? What about Noah? They walked and talked with God" —you're not alone. It's a fair question. And yet, for the moment, let's set aside the debate and focus on the one thing that truly matters: the Savior Himself declared that this was a "first."

And why? Because the Brother of Jared's faith was so unwavering, so absolute, that the veil simply could not hold against it. His knowledge of God became perfect, and when that happens, nothing—not even mortality—can keep a person from the presence of the Lord.

> "Having this perfect knowledge of God, he could not be kept from within the veil. . . . The Lord could not withhold anything from him, for he knew that the Lord could show him all things." **(Ether 3:20, 26)**

That kind of faith is what we should all seek—a faith that refuses to be denied, that presses forward until the Lord Himself cannot help but respond.

For the next several paragraphs the only thing that matters is Jesus Christ says that the brother of Jared was the first man to whom he ever showed Himself. After we discuss this visit, I have included references from several scholars and authorities about the "First" that you will find interesting.

Our goal should be to attain that level of perfect knowledge. My wife once asked how we can know when we reach that level of perfect knowledge. My answer was simple. "You will know when the Savior is standing in front of you." The answer wasn't very satisfactory.

Now, there's a reason this event made it into the "Twelve Days of Christmas." The Lord's statement in Ether 3:15 is striking, even astonishing. It tells us that something about this moment was different, extraordinary. The question of how to reconcile this "first" with previous scriptural accounts is yours to explore. I've gathered insights from scholars and Church authorities that will help, but in the end, what matters most is the event itself—what it teaches us about faith, revelation, and the nature of God.

That's where our focus should be.

Before we get into it here is an interesting tidbit about the brother of Jared.

George Reynolds relates the following interesting incident:

> *While residing in Kirtland, Elder Reynolds Cahoon had a son born to him. One day when President Joseph Smith was passing by his door he called the Prophet in and asked him to bless and the name the baby. Joseph did so and gave the boy the name of Mahonri Moriancumer. When he had finished the blessing he laid the child on the bed, and turning to Elder Cahoon he said, 'the name I have given your son is the name of the brother of Jared; the Lord has just shown (or revealed) it to me.' Elder William F. Cahoon, who was standing near, heard the Prophet make this statement to his father, and this was the first time the name of the brother of Jared was known to the Church in this dispensation.* **(Improvement Era, 8:705)**

Lets look at the events leading up to this special visit.

We know that the Lord had led this little band of Jared's family and friends to the seashore and they had hung out there for 4 years.

> "And it came to pass at the end of four years that the Lord came again unto the brother of Jared, and stood in a cloud and talked with him. And for the space of three hours did the Lord talk with the brother of Jared, and chastened him because he remembered not to call upon the name of the Lord.

And the brother of Jared repented of the evil which he had done,
and did call upon the name of the Lord for his brethren who were
with him. And the Lord said unto him: I will forgive thee and thy
brethren of their sins; but thou shalt not sin any more." (**Ether
2:14-15**)

I have a hard time believing that the Brother of Jared went four whole years
without praying. Maybe he did, but I doubt it. More likely, he was praying—
just not with much intensity or sincerity. Maybe his prayers were rushed,
distracted, half-hearted. Maybe they sounded a lot like mine sometimes.

Eventually, the Lord had enough. He called the Brother of Jared to
repentance, not because He wanted to punish him, but because He wanted
more from him—more faith, more effort, more real connection. And once the
chastisement was over? The Brother of Jared got back on track. And when he
did, his prayers moved mountains—literally.

There is a ton to learn in just these two verses, here are a few;

- We better pray.
- It's a sin not to pray.
- The Lord will forgive us if we fail to pray.
- We better not fail to pray anymore.
- Prayer is a commandment and therefore we should  pray.
- Without prayer we will never see the Lord.

I find this very refreshing and encouraging, considering the fact that Jesus
declared the brother of Jared a sinner but forgave him completely. Completely
enough that shortly thereafter, the brother of Jared stood in the presence of
our Savior.

The most important truth here is simple: prayer is the foundation of faith.
Without it, faith fades. With it, miracles happen.

Here's how it all unfolded for the Brother of Jared:

- After his rebuke, the Lord forgave him. Then, as if nothing had ever
  been amiss, He gave the Brother of Jared detailed instructions for
  building the barges—just as they had done before—to prepare for their
  journey across the great deep.

- The barges were unlike anything we'd expect for ocean travel. They
  were small, light, and sealed tight—built to ride the waves like a whale
  in a storm. Each had a hole on the top and one on the bottom for air, but
  there was a problem: no windows, no light.

- When the Brother of Jared cried out to the Lord about the darkness,
  the Lord didn't hand him an easy answer. Instead, He told him what

wouldn't work—no windows (they'd shatter), no fire (not safe in an enclosed space). Beyond that, the solution was up to him. (**Ether 2:16-25**)

• That's how the Lord works. He doesn't command in all things (**D&C 58:27-28**). He expects us to think, to act, to bring our best ideas to Him.

• So the Brother of Jared did just that. He climbed Mount Shelem, a place so high and steep it demanded both effort and faith, and there he shaped sixteen clear stones from rock—two for each barge. He then carried them to the peak, where he pleaded with the Lord to touch them, to make them shine in the darkness. (**Ether 3:1-5**)

• And the Lord responded. One by one, He reached out and touched the stones with His finger.

• At that moment, the veil lifted from the Brother of Jared's eyes, and he beheld the finger of the Lord. Fear overwhelmed him, and he fell to the ground, afraid that he had seen more than he was permitted.

• The Lord asked why he had fallen. The Brother of Jared, in awe and trembling, explained that he had not known the Lord had flesh and blood.

• When the Lord asked if the Brother of Jared saw more than His finger, and he said he hadn't, the Brother of Jared implored the Redeemer to show Himself to him. The Lord then manifested His body and explained His diving role as Jesus Christ.

• The Lord declared that because of the Brother of Jared's unmatched faith, he had seen what no one before him had: the Lord in His eternal form, prepared from before the foundation of the world to redeem His people. (**Ether 3:6-14**)

• And then the Lord said it—one of the most remarkable statements in scripture: *"Never have I showed myself unto man whom I have created, for never has man believed in me as thou hast."* (**Ether 3:15**)

This was no ordinary day. It was a moment so rare, so sacred, that even the Lord Himself marked it as unique. It was a day when faith shattered barriers, when a mortal man saw God—not because he was commanded to, but because his belief left the Lord with no choice but to reveal Himself.

And that's the kind of faith we should all seek. And I believe Jesus is thrilled when we achieve this level of faith. Imagine what it was like sitting around in heaven and your children are all blabbering in gibberish around a half-finished tower and none of them are sending up coherent prayers and then the Brother of Jared shows some promise. I think our Savior loves to teach and reveal, if we just let Him.

And here is the point that makes this a special day for me.

I can anticipate that my Savior is looking forward to the day when I too will have a perfect knowledge of God and He will visit me. I too can expect total forgiveness if I will but do what it takes.

OK, now here are a few insights from some a little more knowledgeable than I am about this "first" appearing to man.

> Joseph Fielding Smith says this: *CHRIST REVEALED HIMSELF PARTIALLY TO SOME. I have always considered "Ether 3:15 to mean that the Savior stood before the Brother of Jared plainly, distinctly, and showed him his whole body and explained to him that he was a spirit. In his appearance to Adam and Enoch, he had not made himself manifest in such a familiar way. His appearances to earlier prophets had not been with that same fullness.*

The scriptural accounts of talking face to face and of walking with God should not be interpreted in the sense that the Savior stood before those prophets and revealed his whole person. That he may have done so at later periods in the cases of Abraham and Moses is possible, but he had not done so in that fullness in the antediluvian days. For the Brother of Jared he removed the veil completely. He had never showed himself to man before in the manner and way he did to that prophet.

This all makes perfect sense to me but here are some more ways to look at it.

Let me summarize Elder Jeffrey R. Holland's explanation from *Christ and the New Covenant: The Messianic Message of the Book of Mormon.*

In this section, Elder Holland discusses the apparent contradiction between the Lord's statement to the Brother of Jared in Ether 3:15—"Never have I showed myself unto man whom I have created, for never has man believed in me as thou hast."—and earlier scriptural accounts where God appeared to figures like Adam, Enoch, and Noah.

He explains that the key to understanding this passage lies in the Lord's preceding declaration in Ether 3:14, where Christ identifies Himself as the Redeemer who was prepared from the foundation of the world. Elder Holland suggests that while God had indeed appeared to prophets before, the Brother of Jared was the first mortal to see Jesus Christ in His fully revealed, premortal spirit body—not simply as a divine presence or through a vision, but as a tangible, corporeal being.

Elder Holland further clarifies that this moment was unique because of the Brother of Jared's unparalleled faith. His belief was so complete that the veil could not remain intact—he had to see the Lord. The Lord Himself acknowledges that no one before had exercised such faith to bring about such a manifestation.

Now let me lean a bit on Robert L. Millet, a scholar I greatly respect.

> *"We know that the Lord did appear to many of his servants long before his appearance to the brother of Jared. He appeared to Adam and Eve in the Garden of Eden (Moses 4:14-27; Moses 5:4), to Enoch (Moses 7:4, 28-30; Genesis 5:24), to Noah (Moses 8:27; Genesis 6:9), and again to Adam and many of his righteous posterity before the great patriarch's death (D&C 107:53-54).*
>
> *What, therefore, did the Lord mean when he told the brother of Jared that he had never before showed himself unto man whom he had created? Lets consider carefully the Lord's words to the brother of Jared just preceding those in Ether 3:15:*
>
> *Behold, I am he who was prepared from the foundation of the world to redeem my people. Behold, I am Jesus Christ. I am the Father and the Son. In me shall all mankind have light, and that eternally, even they who shall believe on my name; and they shall become my sons and my daughters. (Ether 3:14)*
>
> *Observe that the Lord is talking about those who believe in him. Believers shall have light, eternally, and become his spiritual sons and daughters. Believers are elsewhere called "the sons of God."*
>
> *And Noah and his sons hearkened unto the Lord, and gave heed, and they were called the sons of God. (Moses 8:13)*
>
> *The unbelievers are known as "the sons of men." Mine anger is kindled against the sons of men, for they will not hearken to my voice. (Moses 8:15; Moses 8:14)*
>
> *Now, having explained to the brother of Jared that believers shall become sons and daughters of God (Ether 3:14), the Lord implies in 3:15 a contrast between his course of action with the brother of Jared (a believer) and that with the "sons of men" (unbelievers, carnal men). He appears in person to his servant, a believer, but never in times past has he ever done so to the unbeliever, natural man. Let me present the Lord's words with explanations in brackets to make my meaning clear.*
>
> *And never have I showed myself unto man ["sons of men," unbelievers] whom I have created, for never has man [the unbeliever] believed in me as thou hast. (Ether 3:15)*

This explanation is simple and fits nicely into the context.

Now if my notes are correct, Sidney B. Sperry adds this.

> *"The Lord proceeded to call the brother of Jared's attention to the*

*fact that he and all men were created in his own image; that the
body which he saw was his spirit body, and as he appeared in the
spirit, so would he appear unto his people in the flesh (3:15-16).
The explanation which the Lord gave of his own personality to
the brother of Jared is one of the great contributions the Book of
Mormon makes to this generation. Men need not be in ignorance of
the God they worship. Moroni makes this very pertinent statement:*

*And now, as I, Moroni, said I could not make a full account of these
things which are written, therefore it sufficeth me to say that Jesus
showed himself unto this man in the spirit, even after the manner
and in the likeness of the same body even as he showed himself unto
the Nephites. And he ministered unto him even as he ministered
unto the Nephites; and all this, that this man might know that he
was God, because of the many great works which the Lord had
showed unto him. And because of the knowledge of this man he
could not be kept from beholding within the veil; and he saw the
finger of Jesus, which, when he saw, he fell with fear; for he knew
that it was the finger of the Lord; and he had faith no longer, for he
knew, nothing doubting. Wherefore, having this perfect knowledge
of God, he could not be kept from within the veil; therefore he saw
Jesus; and he did minister unto him. (3:17-20)*

*The Lord commanded the brother of Jared not to permit the great
things which he had seen and heard to go forth unto the world
until the time should come when he would glorify his name in
the flesh. He was to treasure up in his own mind and heart the
things which he had seem and heard; moreover, he was to write
them, but they were to be sealed up, so that no one could interpret
them. The language in which they were to be written, the Lord had
confounded; for that reason he gave two stones (holy interpreters)
to the brother of Jared in order that in his own due time they might
be translated for the benefit of the children of men (3:21-24).*

*Having given these instructions, the Lord showed unto the brother
of Jared all of the inhabitants of the earth, past and future. He
had previously told this prophet and seer that if he would believe
that he could show him all things, it would be done. Because of
Moriancomer's great faith, nothing could be withheld from him. He
must be reckoned one of the greatest men who have ever graced this
planet. These additional things he saw were also to be written down
and were not to be disclosed to men until the Lord so directed. The
brother of Jared was also commanded to seal up the interpreters,
and not show them; the Lord would do this at his own pleasure
(3:25-28).*

*When the brother of Jared came down from the mountain, he wrote down all of the things that the Lord had commanded him. But in accordance with the Lord's command, the younger Mosiah saw to it that they should not come unto the knowledge of the world until after Christ should show himself unto his people. After the Christ came in person among his people, he commanded the writings of the brother of Jared to be made manifest. Moroni wrote down upon the sealed plates-later in possession of the Prophet Joseph Smith-the very things which the brother of Jared had recorded, and he indicates that there never were greater manifestations given to man than were given to the great Jaredite prophet. The Lord directed Moroni to seal up these great writings along with the interpreters (Urim and Thummim). (4:1-5) "*

*In 4:6-19 we find a revelation mainly concerning the Gentiles which was received by Moroni from the Lord.*

*In these verses, the Lord makes known that the great visions which the brother of Jared saw shall not come forth unto mankind until the Gentiles repent of their iniquity and become clean before the Lord. When the day comes that the people exercise faith in Christ, then will the Lord manifest to mankind all the things which the brother of Jared saw. In fact, all of the revelations of God will be given unto man. Those who contend against God's word shall be accursed, and he will not show them greater things than have hitherto been given. The Lord pleads with the Gentiles to come unto him and receive the greater revelations which have been hidden away because of unbelief (4:13). He also admonishes the house of Israel to come unto him. He tells them that when they call upon the Father in his name with a broken and a contrite spirit, then shall they know that the Father has remembered the covenants which he made with their ancestors. Then the revelations of John the Beloved will be unfolded before the eyes of all the people. Following this, the Savior proceeds to call upon all the ends of the earth to come unto him, to believe in his gospel, and to be baptized in his name. Those who believe and are baptized will be saved, but those who believe not will be condemned.*

*These admonitions of the Lord are of real interest because they indicate the great spiritual character of Moroni. The channel of revelation was open to him; without it we should have been deprived of great words from the Savior himself."*

Moroni was writing at least twenty-five hundred years after the experience of the brother of Jared (depending on when one dates the Jaredites, which I will not attempt here) and about four centuries after Christ's coming to Lehi's children.

Joseph Fielding Smith, Doctrines of Salvation, comp. Bruce R. McConkie, 3 vols. (Salt Lake City: Bookcraft, 1954-56), 1:37. See also Joseph Fielding Smith, Answers to Gospel Questions, 5 vols. (Salt Lake City: Deseret Book Co., 1957-66), 2:123-26.

Bruce R. McConkie, The Promised Messiah: The First Coming of Christ (Salt Lake City: Deseret Book Co., 1978), 599-600.

# THE SIXTH DAY OF CHRISTMAS

*"Glad Tidings of Great Joy"*

## The Birth of Jesus Christ

One recurring theme throughout the scriptures in the many prophecies of the Savior is the phrase "Glad Tidings and Great Joy."

Here are just a few of the many that tell us the coming of our Savior is great news.

- And the angel answering said unto him, I am Gabriel, that stand in the presence of God; and am sent to speak unto thee, and to shew thee these glad tidings. (Luke 1: 19)

- And now, my son, I would say somewhat unto you concerning the coming of Christ. Behold, I say unto you, that it is he that surely shall come to take away the sins of the world; yea, he cometh to declare glad tidings of salvation unto his people.  And now, my son, this was the ministry unto which ye were called, to declare these glad tidings unto this people, to prepare their minds; or rather that salvation might come unto them, that they may prepare the minds of their children to hear the word at the time of his coming. (Alma 39: 15-16, 19)

- Yea, and the voice of the Lord, by the mouth of angels, doth declare it unto all nations; yea, doth declare it, that they may have glad tidings of great joy; yea, and he doth sound these glad tidings among all his people, yea, even to them that are scattered abroad upon the face of the earth;  wherefore they have come unto us. (Alma 13: 22- 23)

- And he said unto me: Awake, and hear the words which I shall tell thee; for behold, I am come to declare unto you the glad tidings of great joy. (Mosiah 3: 3)

- And angels did appear unto men, wise men, and did declare unto them glad tidings of great joy; thus in this year the scriptures began to be fulfilled. (Hel. 16: 14)

The angels and prophets did not speak their own words—they declared the words given to them by the Savior Himself. That's why the message remains so consistent. So what are these "glad tidings" that bring such great joy? A simple reading makes it clear: the glad tidings are that Christ will come. He will be born into mortality, willingly leave His heavenly throne, take upon Himself a body of flesh and blood, and then—through His infinite love—lay down that body in death, only to take it up again in resurrection. In doing so, He redeems His people. This is the message of hope, the message that should fill our hearts with joy.

This is the kind of faith that changes people, that shapes behavior and determines destiny. The Savior's mortal mission was singular in purpose: to bring about our immortality and eternal life. Everything between His birth and resurrection was the how—the demonstration of His gospel, showing us how to live, what to become, and how to fully receive the power of His Atonement in our own lives.

All prophecy, all history, every person who ever looked forward with hope—all of it hinged on those 34 years of Christ's mortal ministry. No event in the history of the world was more anticipated. His birth meant the fulfillment of thousands of years of prophecy. It marked the end of the Law of Moses and the beginning of His Church. It ushered in the reinstitution of His gospel. And, of course, it set in motion the events that would lead to His willing sacrifice and triumphant resurrection.

It's no wonder that Satan tried so desperately to stop Him. Herod slaughtered thousands of innocent children in an attempt to prevent His mission. When that failed, Satan himself tempted Christ. When that too failed, Satan turned the hearts of men against Him, leading to the moment when the Son of God made the ultimate choice—to lay down His life for those very men who sought to destroy Him.

Even if we set aside the incomprehensible suffering of Gethsemane and Calvary, just the reality of His birth and mortal life is worthy of our deepest reverence. This is the King of Kings who left the courts on high, who stepped down from His divine throne to be born in the humblest of circumstances. What earthly prince would ever leave his palace, live among beggars, endure their scorn, and then willingly give his life to save them? The very thought stretches the limits of my understanding. And yet, He did it. He came. And because of that, we have every reason to rejoice.

To me, the greatness of Christ's birth isn't just the event itself—it's the condescension. His willingness to step down, to leave His throne and enter mortality to fulfill His sacred duty. That alone is staggering. But beyond that, the story of Christ's birth is also the story of His earthly parents—Mary and Joseph. I am in absolute awe when I think about them.

President Gordon B. Hinckley once said that most children just grow up to become people. As a father, I, of course, think my children are wonderful, but I can't begin to imagine what it would be like to be told that my child would grow up to be the Savior of the world—my personal Savior. The Creator of heaven and earth. My Judge. As His mother and stepfather, how do you even keep perspective with that knowledge? What kind of faith, what kind of obedience, what kind of love did Mary and Joseph have to be entrusted with raising the Son of God? I can't wait to read their full history one day.

And then there's the Savior Himself. As we've discussed, the angel Gabriel was part of the divine preparation, but to me, the story of Christmas is Christ's willingness to step down.

We have the nativity story, the shepherds, the wise men, and all the beautiful details that go with it. But let's think about His perspective. What was happening with Jesus before that night in Bethlehem? Was He just absent for nine months? Or was He, in His divine capacity, still fully engaged in the work of salvation? We know He was eager to come. Look at what He said to Nephi—this was the real beginning of it all:

> "On the morrow come I into the world, to show unto the world
> that I will fulfill all that which I have caused to be spoken by the
> mouth of my holy prophets." (3 **Nephi** 1:13)

He didn't just say He was coming—He said He was coming to show the world. Up to that point, He had already won a war in heaven, created the earth, cast Adam and Eve out of the Garden, and both punished and rewarded His children. But now? Now it was time to step in and show us.

All throughout the Old Testament and the Book of Mormon, prophets had foretold His coming. And as He told Nephi, He was the one who caused those prophecies to be given in the first place. This wasn't an afterthought. The details were laid out from the very beginning. His birth was the fulfillment of thousands of years of promises, prophecies, and divine preparation. And when the time came, He didn't hesitate. He stepped down. For us.

In the Book or Mormon, Nephi records this glorious day as follows.

> 4 And it came to pass that in the commencement of the ninety
> and second year, behold, the prophecies of the prophets began
> to be fulfilled more fully; for there began to be greater signs and
> greater miracles wrought among the people.

> 5 But there were some who began to say that the time was past
> for the words to be fulfilled, which were spoken by Samuel, the
> Lamanite.

> 6 And they began to rejoice over their brethren, saying: Behold

the time is past, and the words of Samuel are not fulfilled; therefore, your joy and your faith concerning this thing hath been vain.

7  And it came to pass that they did make a great uproar throughout the land; and the people who believed began to be very sorrowful, lest by any means those things which had been spoken might not come to pass.

8 But behold, they did watch steadfastly for that day and that night and that day which should be as one day as if there were no night, that they might know that their faith had not been vain.

9 Now it came to pass that there was a day set apart by the unbelievers, that all those who believed in those traditions should be put to death except the sign should come to pass, which had been given by Samuel the prophet.

10 Now it came to pass that when Nephi, the son of Nephi, saw this wickedness of his people, his heart was exceedingly sorrowful.

11 And it came to pass that he went out and bowed himself down upon the earth, and cried mightily to his God in behalf of his people, yea, those who were about to be destroyed because of their faith in the tradition of their fathers.

12 And it came to pass that he cried mightily unto the Lord all that day; and behold, the voice of the Lord came unto him, saying:

13 Lift up your head and be of good cheer; for behold, the time is at hand, and on this night shall the sign be given, and on the morrow come I into the world, to show unto the world that I will fulfil all that which I have caused to be spoken by the mouth of my holy prophets.

14 Behold, I come unto my own, to fulfill all things which I have made known unto the children of men from the foundation of the world, and to do the will, both of the Father and of the Son—of the Father because of me, and of the Son because of my flesh. And behold, the time is at hand, and this night shall the sign be given.

15 And it came to pass that the words which came unto Nephi were fulfilled, according as they had been spoken; for behold, at the going down of the sun there was no darkness; and the people began to be astonished because there was no darkness when the night came. (3 Nephi 1:4 - 15)

He gave the prophets their words—He told them exactly what to prophesy. He knew precisely what would happen and exactly when.

To me, that is incredibly comforting. Think about it—every prophecy about His first coming was fulfilled down to the smallest detail. Now, look at the prophecies of His Second Coming and the revelations He has given to His prophets and apostles about our day. I have absolute confidence that, no matter how chaotic the world gets, we ridiculous mortals aren't going to derail His divine plan.

# THE SEVENTH DAY OF CHRISTMAS

*"Follow me, and I will make you fishers of men."*

## The calling of Peter, James and John.

Of all the cool days in the Savior's ministry—days filled with miracles, profound teachings, and acts of divine power—why would I count this one among the twelve greatest? A simple day, a stroll along the lakeshore, a few words spoken to fishermen and tax collectors. No grand miracle, no heavenly signs*. And yet, this day changed everything—not just for those twelve men, but for the entire world.

*If we follow Luke's account, then Peter, James, and John were called as disciples on the same day as the miracle of the fishes, thus it would not have been an ordinary day. However, Matthew and Mark suggest that their calling may have been a separate moment from their first encounter with Jesus. Either way, the miracle confirmed for them that Jesus was no ordinary teacher and led them to leave everything behind to follow Him.

I take a little liberty here (no surprise) and extend this day to include what followed: the establishment of Christ's Church both on earth and in the spirit world. Because without this day, without the Apostles, the Restoration would have had nothing to restore.

Nephi saw it. Long before the Savior walked the shores of Galilee, Nephi was shown a vision of Christ and those who followed Him:

"And I also beheld twelve others following him." (1 Nephi 11:29)

And then the angel explained:

"Thou rememberest the Twelve Apostles of the Lamb? Behold they are they who shall judge the twelve tribes of Israel." (1 Nephi 12:9)

And what would their role be?

"These last records, which thou hast seen among the Gentiles, shall establish the truth of the first, which are of the twelve apostles of the Lamb, and shall make known the plain and precious things which have been taken away…that the Lamb of God is the Son of the Eternal Father, and the Savior of the world." (1 Nephi 13:40)

These three verses in 1 Nephi validate for me that the calling of His Apostles was an event of grave importance. The angel showed Nephi that the calling of the Twelve was not just an incidental event. It was a moment of eternal significance, one that shaped the future of Christ's work. The Lord knew that His Atonement needed a means by which it would be taught to the world. He knew that people would need structure, guidance, and authorized servants to preach His word. So He called the Twelve. He gave them power and authority. He prepared them to carry His gospel forward after He was gone. They will do many things but mostly, their work will "make known to all kindreds, tongues, and people, that the Lamb of God is the Son of the Eternal Father, and the Savior of the world"

Without the establishment of His Church, how would we recognize His truth today? If He had not set this pattern, what exactly would have been restored in 1820? Christ did not leave His followers without direction. The establishment of His organized church during His mortal ministry set a pattern that was essential for the protection of His doctrine following His death as well as the establishment of His earthly kingdom in the latter- days. Without this, including His authority and guidance, we today would be lost. His great sacrifice would be of no use. What would have been restored in 1820? What law would we be living now? How would we recognize His church? If He really did not need a structured way for us to live and return to Him, why would He have had the Mosaic Law? Why would He have had fulfilled it and called Apostles to whom He gave keys and authority?

The Savior spent a lot of time with the organization of His church. It must have been very important to Him. This is why this day was a big deal for me. He organized. He ordained. He gave keys.

This is why the day He called His Apostles matters so much. It was not just a lakeside conversation—it was the foundation of everything that followed. It was the day He ensured that His work would go forth to all the world, not just in His lifetime, but for all generations to come.

And because of that, His church has shaped my life.

Consider how often the Apostles found themselves contending with the Jews about the Mosaic Law, even after Christ had fulfilled it. The debates were constant, the resistance fierce. Why? Because the world needed clarity. It needed structure. It needed authorized servants to preach, teach, exhort, and protect the truth. Without them, the gospel message would have been lost in confusion and contradiction.

And He did not stop with the living.

Peter tells us what the Savior was doing in the days between His death and resurrection:

> "For for this cause was the gospel preached also to them that are dead, that they might be judged according to men in the flesh, but live according to God in the spirit." (1 Peter 4:6)

The Savior was at work among the spirits, establishing His kingdom there just as He had on earth. Modern revelation confirms that this was not a disorganized effort—it was an organized work, directed by Christ Himself.

The New Testament gives us powerful testimonies of Christ's death and resurrection, but only glimpses of where His spirit was in the meantime. Peter offers a clue (1 Peter 3:18–19), and modern revelation fills in the rest. The Savior did not waste a moment.

Peter doesn't go into detail about how this work was organized, but let's think about it. Would the Savior stand before the entire host of departed souls and deliver one grand sermon, leaving them to figure it out on their own? That's not how He operated in mortality, and modern revelation confirms it's not how He operates in the spirit world either. His work is organized. His doctrine is safeguarded. His messengers continue their labor beyond the veil.

The New Testament gives us four powerful testimonies of Christ's Crucifixion and Resurrection, but only brief glimpses of where His spirit was in the time between (see 1 Peter 3:18–19; 1 Peter 4:6). The Restoration fills in the picture. The Savior's mission did not pause. He was still teaching, still organizing, still ensuring that His gospel would reach every soul— living and dead.

> *"Modern revelation fills the void with the revelation given through President Joseph F. Smith pertaining to the spirit world (D&C 138). Here we learn the remarkable mission of the Redeemer to the righteous spirits who had "departed the mortal life, firm in the hope of a glorious resurrection" (D&C 138:14).*

> *During those three days, the Savior "organized his forces and appointed messengers, clothed with power and authority, and commissioned them to go forth and carry the light of the gospel to them that were in darkness, even to all the spirits of men; and thus was the gospel preached to the dead" (D&C 138:30).*

> *This revelation is an essential chapter in the study of the Savior's*

Here are a few key elements that I think are fundamental in Christ setting up His church.

In James Talmage's book "Articles of Faith" he makes it very clear that to have Christ call His apostles and give them authority was not a new thing by any means. I summarize what James Talmage taught about authority.

One of the most inspiring truths of the restored gospel is the perfect order that characterizes the Church of Jesus Christ. The Lord has always been deliberate about how His work is carried out. Those who minister in sacred ordinances must be called of God and commissioned by proper authority. That's not a recent idea—it's an eternal pattern.

You'd be hard-pressed to find a single example in scripture where someone claimed authority on their own and had the Lord honor that ministry. In fact, the opposite is usually true. Over and over again, the Lord's pattern is clear— He calls His servants.

Just look at Noah and Enoch, both of whom found grace in the eyes of the Lord. Abraham, Isaac, and Jacob were called by the voice of God. Moses didn't choose his role—he was called. And when his time was nearly over, Moses didn't leave succession to chance. He went to the Lord, and the Lord named Joshua, son of Nun, for that sacred task. The pattern continues with Aaron and his sons, divinely chosen from among Israel to minister in the priest's office.

Samuel's story has always struck me. Chosen as a boy, called by name, and set apart to speak for God—to command, to bless, and even to rebuke kings. There was no mistaking the authority behind Samuel's words. And that pattern stretches from prophet to prophet.

The Lord Jesus Christ followed the same order during His mortal ministry. He didn't invite apostles casually. He called them. He ordained them. And after His Resurrection, He appeared to the remaining eleven and gave them specific commissions to move the work forward.

After the Savior's ascension, the same pattern of calling by divine authority continued. Matthias was chosen to replace Judas—not by popular vote, but by revelation and sacred lot. Saul of Tarsus—later Paul—wasn't just converted by a heavenly vision; he was also formally ordained and set apart for his unique mission.

You and I declare our belief in this order every time we recite the fifth Article of Faith: "We believe that a man must be called of God, by prophecy, and by the laying on of hands by those who are in authority, to preach the gospel and administer in the ordinances thereof." That principle has never changed.

Even when scripture doesn't explicitly mention hands being laid on a man's head, the pattern is so consistent that I believe we can safely say that's how the Lord has always done it. The priesthood has always been passed down through righteous lineage and divine commission.

Adam laid his hands on Enos. Enos ordained Mahalaleel. Jared, Enoch, Methuselah—each received their authority under the hands of those who held it before them. Noah was ordained by Methuselah. Melchizedek, who conferred the priesthood on Abraham, had received it through that same sacred chain. Esaias, a contemporary of Abraham, was ordained by the hand of God. From Esaias to Gad, then to Jeremy, Elihu, Caleb, and finally to Jethro—who ordained Moses. And when the Lord told Moses to prepare Joshua, Moses laid his hands on him. The pattern is clear.

And that's the beauty of this gospel. The line of priesthood authority is not only traceable—it's unbroken. It is as consistent and intentional as the God who gave it.

What this means is that Christ left no room for doubt—He has a clear, deliberate plan for the organization of His church. And at the heart of that plan is authority. A testimony comes by the Spirit, but there is great comfort in knowing that the Lord has established an order, a pattern, a way to ensure that His work is done His way.

Now, if Joseph Smith had made all of this up, we'd have to admit—he was nothing short of a genius. To create a system so perfectly aligned with the patterns found in scripture, so deeply rooted in both ancient and modern revelation, and so seamlessly designed to stand the test of time? That would be remarkable. But the reality is far simpler, and far more profound: he didn't make it up. He restored what was always there.

Let me now include James Talmadge's own words.

> *"In the days of the apostles circumstances rendered it expedient to appoint special officers in the Church, to care for the poor and attend to the distribution of supplies; these were selected with care and were set apart through prayer and laying on of hands. Timothy was similarly ordained, as witness the admonitions given him by Paul: "Neglect not the gift that is in thee, which was given thee*

*by prophecy, with the laying on of the hands of the presbytery,"
and again, "Stir up the gift of God, which is in thee by the putting
on of my hands." The Lord has bound Himself by covenant to
acknowledge the acts of His authorized servants. Unto whomsoever
the elders of the Church give promise after acceptable baptism, the
Holy Ghost will come. Whatever the Priesthood shall bind or loose
on earth, in accordance with the Lord's commands, is to be bound
or loosed in heaven; the sick upon whom the elders lay their hands
are to recover; and many other signs are to follow them that believe.
So jealous is the Lord of the power to officiate in His name, that
at the judgment all who have aided or persecuted His servants are
to be rewarded or punished as if they had done those things unto
Himself."*

James E. Talmage's The Articles of Faith, typically around
pages 184–200 (depending on the printing), or in the
section under "Authority in the Ministry" / "Ordination to
the Ministry" / "The Authorized Imposition of Hands."

*"Scriptures also make it clear that Unauthorized Ministrations in
priesthood functions are not just invalid, but they also sinful. In His
dealings with mankind God recognizes and honors the Priesthood
established by His direction, and does not like unauthorized
assumption of authority. A lesson is taught by the case of Korah
and his associates, in their rebellion against the authority of the
Priesthood in that they falsely professed the right to minister in the
priest's office. The Lord promptly visited them for their sins, causing
the ground to cleave asunder and to swallow them up with all their
belongings.*

*Consider also the affliction that fell upon Miriam, the sister of
Moses, a prophetess among the people. She, with Aaron, railed
against Moses, and they said: "Hath the Lord indeed spoken only
by Moses? Hath he not spoken also by us? And the Lord heard
it." Jehovah came down in a cloud and stood in the door of the
tabernacle, denouncing their presumption and vindicating the
authority of His oracle, Moses. When the cloud passed from the
tabernacle Miriam was seen to be leprous, white as snow; and
according to the law she was shut out from the camp of Israel.
However, through the earnest entreaties of Moses, the Lord healed
the woman and she was subsequently permitted to return to the
company.*

*Consider the fate of Uzza, the Israelite who met sudden death
through the anger of God because he put forth his hand to steady*

Christ didn't just establish His church while He walked the earth—He made it unmistakably clear who held the authority to lead it. That authority wasn't meant to be scattered, debated, or seized by those without divine commission. It was given, carefully and deliberately, to those He called. So, when the time came for His church to be restored, it only made sense that those who had been entrusted with that authority in the beginning would return to restore it again.

No one officiates in the sacred ordinances of The Church of Jesus Christ of Latter-day Saints without being properly ordained by those who hold the necessary authority. That's not just a preference—it's a law of heaven. Priesthood authority is always passed from one who holds it to another, linking every bearer of that priesthood today back to Joseph Smith, who received it under the hands of Peter, James, and John—who, in turn, had been ordained by the Savior Himself.

A few years ago, our Young Men's organization decided to trace the priesthood lineage of every young man and leader in the ward. We followed each line of authority, name by name, generation by generation, back to its origins. And without fail, every single one of them could trace their priesthood back to Jesus Christ. Every one. Now, I don't know of a single minister, pastor, priest, or religious leader in any other church who can say the same.

That is a profound claim. But more than that, it's a profound reality.

One of the things I love about the way the Savior established His Church—deliberately, with clear organization and authority—is that it allows us to recognize it today. The pattern He set wasn't just for His time; it was for all time. Because He is the same yesterday, today, and forever, His Church would be, too.

> *""The Gospel of Jesus Christ is the everlasting Gospel; its principles, laws and ordinances, and the Church organization founded thereon, must be ever the same. In searching for the true Church, therefore, one must look for an organization comprising the offices established of old, the callings of apostles, prophets, evangelists, high priests, seventies, pastors, bishops, elders, priests, teachers, deacons—not men bearing these names merely, but ministers able to vindicate their claim to position as officers in the Lord's service, through the evidences of power and authority accompanying their ministry."*

James Talmage – Articles of Faith

The actual organization of the church as we know it in the latter-days has not however, always been on the earth. The need for authority has been and will always be, but here a few things that I found very interesting.

The Church before the Birth of Christ—It is a significant fact that the word "church" does not appear in our English version of the Old Testament. From the time of Moses to the coming of Christ the people lived under the jurisdiction of the Law, between which and the Gospel, as embodied in the Church established by Jesus Christ, there is important distinction. Among the Nephites, however, who were sequestered on the western continent, the Church did exist as an organized body prior to the advent of the Lord Jesus Christ.

If we read in the Book of Moses we learn but little of a church organization but we see there was a proper process of the passing of authority.

> "And thus the Gospel began to be preached, from the beginning, being declared by holy angels sent forth from the presence of God, and by his own voice, and by the gift of the Holy Ghost.
>
> And thus all things were confirmed unto Adam, by an holy ordinance, and the Gospel preached, and a decree sent forth, that it should be in the world, until the end thereof; and thus it was. Amen." Moses 5:58 - 59

The Doctrine and Covenants outlines priesthood authority as well.

> 6 And the sons of Moses, according to the Holy Priesthood which

he received under the hand of his father-in-law, Jethro;

7 And Jethro received it under the hand of Caleb;

8 And Caleb received it under the hand of Elihu;

9 And Elihu under the hand of Jeremy;

10 And Jeremy under the hand of Gad;

11 And Gad under the hand of Esaias;

12 And Esaias received it under the hand of God.

13 Esaias also lived in the days of Abraham, and was blessed of him—

14 Which Abraham received the priesthood from Melchizedek, who received it through the lineage of his fathers, even till Noah;

15 And from Noah till Enoch, through the lineage of their fathers;

16 And from Enoch to Abel, who was slain by the conspiracy of his brother, who received the priesthood by the commandments of God, by the hand of his father Adam, who was the first man—

17 Which priesthood continueth in the church of God in all generations, and is without beginning of days or end of years.

18 And the Lord confirmed a priesthood also upon Aaron and his seed, throughout all their generations, which priesthood also continueth and abideth forever with the priesthood which is after the holiest order of God.

19 And this greater priesthood administereth the gospel and holdeth the key of the mysteries of the kingdom, even the key of the knowledge of God.

20 Therefore, in the ordinances thereof, the power of godliness is manifest.

21 And without the ordinances thereof, and the authority of the priesthood, the power of godliness is not manifest unto men in the flesh;

22 For without this no man can see the face of God, even the Father, and live.

23 Now this Moses plainly taught to the children of Israel in the wilderness, and sought diligently to sanctify his people that they might behold the face of God; (D & C 84:6-23)

Moses "sought diligently" to prepare his people to see the face of God. As we know they rejected the invitation and lost the opportunity and thus had to live under the "Law" rather than the fullness of the Gospel of Jesus Christ.

The records that we have of the initial calling being extended by the Savior are found in three of the four Gospels: Mathew, Mark and John. The actual records are brief so I have included them here:

> "And Jesus, walking by the sea of Galilee, saw two brethren, Simon called Peter, and Andrew his brother, casting a net into the sea: for they were fishers. And he saith unto them, Follow me, and I will make you fishers of men.  And they straightway left their nets, and followed him. And going on from thence, he saw other two brethren, James the son of Zebedee, and John his brother, in a ship with Zebedee their father, mending their nets; and he called them.  And they immediately left the ship and their father, and followed him. " Matt 4:28-22

> " Now as he walked by the sea of Galilee, he saw Simon and Andrew his brother casting a net into the sea: for they were fishers. And Jesus said unto them, Come ye after me, and I will make you to become fishers of men.

> And straightway they forsook their nets, and followed him. And when he had gone a little further thence, he saw James the son of Zebedee, and John his brother, who also were in the ship mending their nets.

> And straightway he called them: and they left their father Zebedee in the ship with the hired servants, and went after him." Mark 1:16-20

The lesson to me in these few verses apart from the entire church organization stuff just discussed, are two fold:

1) Christ called these men to follow Him – a simple invitation, the same invitation He has issued to me, and

2) "straightway they forsook their nets, and followed Him – which is exactly what I better do.

Another thing that is wonderful in this whole process of the Savior selecting apostles and prophets both anciently and in our day is the fact that I now have an absolute source of truth, special witnesses of our Savior, Apostles of the Lord Jesus Christ.

# The Eighth Day of Christmas

*"Glory be to the Father, and I partook and finished my preparations unto the children of men."*

**The Atonement of Jesus Christ.**

Of all the days in the twelve we focus on in this book, there are none more sacred or significant than day eight and nine of these twelve days that changed everything. Those days began with a week that was unlike any other in human history.

I've had my share of demanding weeks—periods when everything I had to offer was called for. But no week in any mortal life, no matter how intense or exhausting, can compare to the week the Savior endured. For me, hard weeks usually end with a bit of rest when the weekend arrives. But for Him, that week ended with the ultimate offering—His very life.

When I reflect on the final days of the Savior's earthly ministry, I'm overcome by the sheer depth and purpose packed into each moment. From His triumphal entry into Jerusalem to His quiet suffering in Gethsemane, from the betrayal and scourging, to the cross and the tomb—every act was intentional, every step sacred.

## The Week That Changed Eternity

In studying the final days of the Savior's mortal ministry, I've come to see not only the order of events but the divine purpose guiding each moment. This was not just a significant week in history—it was the week. Every step the Savior took led deliberately to the Atonement. It was a week filled with miracles, parables, prophecy, and confrontation, culminating in the ultimate offering: His perfect life.

## Saturday Evening – The Anointing

The week began quietly—with love and reverence. On Saturday evening, the night before entering Jerusalem, Jesus dined with close friends. It was here that Mary anointed His feet with costly oil. Some complained, but the Savior accepted her gift as sacred. She knew, perhaps better than any, what was coming. That act prepared Him for burial before anyone else fully understood (probably including Mary) what He meant by saying His time was at hand.

## Sunday – Palm Sunday

The world now calls it Palm Sunday, and rightly so. Jesus rode into Jerusalem on a donkey—the ancient symbol of Jewish royalty. Zechariah had foretold it (Zech. 9:9), and the people rejoiced with palm branches and praises. The Romans saw no threat; they misunderstood what kind of King He was. But those who should have understood—the Jewish leaders—tried to stop it.

> "Master, rebuke thy disciples," they said. And the Lord, with divine power in His voice, replied, "I tell you, if these should hold their peace, the stones would immediately cry out." (Luke 19:40; see also Hab. 2:11)

Later that day, Greeks sought Him out, and He taught a powerful truth:

> "Except a corn of wheat fall into the ground and die, it abideth alone." (John 12:24)

His life, like that grain, would soon be buried—only to bring forth life for all of us.

Then came the voice from Heaven, heard by all present. Some thought it thundered. But the Father was strengthening His Son for what lay ahead. (John 12:27–36; Jesus the Christ, pg. 520) Afterward, Jesus returned to Bethany to rest.

## Monday – Power and Purity

On the way back into Jerusalem, Jesus passed a fig tree—full of leaves but bearing no fruit. He cursed it. Some wondered why. But I believe it was a powerful teaching moment—a warning against hypocrisy, and a reminder of His authority not only to give life, but also to take it. (Matt. 21:18–22; Mark 11:12–14)

Then came the cleansing of the temple. Again. This time He called it "My house". That one phrase enraged the chief priests and scribes. They thought they owned the temple, but the true Master had returned. And then—how beautiful this moment must have been—the children sang: "Hosanna to the Son of David." (Matt. 21:15, 16; Psalm 8:2)

Out of the mouths of babes, the truth rang out. The leaders couldn't stand it. But the Savior let it stand. Then, once more, He left the city for Bethany.

## Tuesday – Authority, Parables, and Final Public Teachings

Tuesday brought confrontation and clarity.

The disciples passed the same fig tree—and now it was withered and dead. A living symbol of what happens when outward appearances mask inner emptiness. (Mark 11:20–26)

Once in Jerusalem, the Savior was challenged again: "By what authority doest thou these things?" And He answered, not with a defensive statement, but with a question they dared not answer—about the baptism of John. (Matt. 21:23–27)

Then, knowing His time was short, Jesus taught three powerful final parables:

- The Two Sons – One son says "no" but repents and obeys. The other says "yes" but does nothing. (Matt. 21:28–32) Which are we?

- The Wicked Husbandmen – A vivid prophecy of His rejection, suffering, and death. (Matt. 21:33–41)

- The Royal Marriage Feast – A call to heed the invitation of the King, and a warning not to take it lightly. (Matt. 22:1–14; see Luke 14:16–24 and Jesus the Christ, pg. 538)

These were His last public parables. The final symbolic sermons of the Savior, offered not in quiet corners but boldly, in the face of growing opposition. (See Jesus the Christ, pg. 540)

And so the week continued. Each day drawing Him nearer to Gethsemane. Nearer to the Cross. And nearer to the moment when love would conquer death.

More to come, but oh, what a beginning to the greatest week in the history of the world.

Probably Tuesday afternoon. Foolish leaders trying again – Pharisees and Herodians Matt 22:15-22 Mark 12: 13-17 Luke 20:19-26 "Is it lawful to pay tribute unto Ceasar?" They really kissed up first and then offered this trick question. Even after this evidence of His loyalty to the law of the land, they still told Pilot that Christ was forbidding to give tribute unto Caesar.

Another try, this time by the Sadducees. No bodily resurrection. Story about seven brothers and one wife. Matt 22:23-33 Mark 12: 18-27 Luke 20:27-38 The Pharisees loved this because they hated the Sadducees. Then they plugged ahead with "Master, which is the great commandment?" Matt 22:34-40, Mark 12:28-34. This questioner actually admitted the truth and Christ said "Thou art not far from the kingdom if God." We don't know if the one that posed this question actually changed and followed the Savior. Usually it mentions that they went away angry etc. This time it didn't.

Sadducees, Herodians, Pharisees, Lawyers and Scribes had all challenged and failed. "No man after that durst ask him an question." At this point Jesus went after them – Matt 22:41-46 Mark 12: 35-37 Luke 20:41-44

"What think ye of Christ? Whose son is he? They said "the son of David." This exchange really was Jesus' way of putting it all into context. Jesus was Jehovah, Lord and God, before David, Abraham or Adam was known on the earth. And he was in the lineage of David. Just a little condemnation to the very foolish group of Jewish leaders.

Speaking to the disciples but so that the Scribes and Pharisees could hear he told the disciples what to do. Matt 23 Mark 12: 38-40 Luke 20:45-47 11:39-52 Pg 553 Jesus The Christ by James Talmage 554-560.

"But woe unto you, Scribes and Pharisees, hypocrites!" You won't go into heaven nor will you let others in.

"But woe unto you, Scribes and Pharisees, hypocrites!" Ye devour widows' houses and for pretense make long prayer .

"But woe unto you, Scribes and Pharisees, hypocrites!" Ye compass land and sea to get a convert then you pervert him. Out of a bad heathen they made a worse Jew.

"But woe unto you, Scribes and Pharisees, hypocrites!" Swear by the temple, Swear by the gold of the temple.

"But woe unto you, Scribes and Pharisees, hypocrites!" Ye pay tithe of mint and anise and cumin and omitted the weightier matters.

"But woe unto you, Scribes and Pharisees, hypocrites!" Ye make clean the outside of the cup and leave the stuff inside full of extortion and excess.

"But woe unto you, Scribes and Pharisees, hypocrites!" Ye are like whited sepulchers beautiful on the outside but full of dead bones and rotting flesh inside.

"But woe unto you, Scribes and Pharisees, hypocrites!" Ye build tombs for the prophets and say you would have been different you are just as bad.

Jesus' lamentation over Jerusalem – Matt 23:37-39 Luke 13:34-35. This was kind of un-dedicating the temple. He calls it your house.

The widows mite. Mark 12:41-44, Luke 21:1-4

Final withdrawal from the temple - John 12:42-50. They wouldn't believe because of fear of the praise of man. If you believe in me you believe in the Father – this is the call to believe.

Prediction of the destruction of the temple – Matt 24:1,2, Mark 13:1, 2 Luke 21: 5,6 "Not one stone left upon another."

Signs of the times from the Mount of Olives – the disciples asked about the previous predictions earlier in the Temple. The lesson is – what does this mean to me – we shouldn't be deceived and we better be ready. Mark 13:11, Luke 21:19 "But of that day and that hour knoweth no man, no, not the angles which are in heaven, neither the Son, but the Father." Mark 13:31? The Apostles are told they are the stewards and they better watch. We are those stewards – Matt 24:45-51, We are those stewards now.

Parable of the 10 virgins – Matt 25:1-13

**Tuesday evening** – Parable of the Entrusted talents – Matt 25:14-30. We have no ownership – we are only stewards and we are held accountable. Notice that the servant that lost everything blamed the failure on fear of the Lord saying that the Lord is a bad guy.

This was the final parable.

Matt 25:31-46 When the Lord comes the wheat will be divided from the tares. – Inasmuch as ye have done it unto one of the least of these and not unto one of the least of these you have done it unto me.

Walking back from Olive toward Bethany,

> "Ye know, that after two days is the feast of the Passover, and the
> Son of man is betrayed to be crucified." (Matt 26:2)

At this point it got a little hard to pin the timing and days together, I have always had a question about the actual day of Crucifixion being on Friday. It probably was, but here is my question – Since we are told that he laid in the tomb three days and He taught in the spirit world three days and in the new world there were three days of darkness, does from late Friday afternoon, all day Saturday and a few hours in the pre-dawn Sunday count as three days?

That does not seem to me to be three days. However there are dozens of references to His rising on the "third" day so maybe "three days" is only a matter of semantics –

> "From that time forth began Jesus to shew unto his disciples, how
> that he must go unto Jerusalem, and suffer many things of the
> elders and chief priests and scribes, and be killed, and be raised
> again the third day." Matt. 16: 21.

If we read some of the references from the Book of Mormon where they had three days of darkness, it does not necessarily clear it up. Judge for yourself.

> "In that day that he shall suffer death," was the prophetic word; "the sun shall be darkened and refuse to give his light unto you; and also the moon and the stars; and there shall be no light upon the face of this land, even from the time that he shall suffer death, for the space of three days, to the time that he shall rise again from the dead." (Hel. 14:20.)

> "And it came to pass that it did last for the space of three days that there was no light seen; and there was great mourning and howling and weeping among all the people continually; yea, great were the groanings of the people, because of the darkness and the great destruction which had come upon them." 3 Nephi 8:23

> "And the God of our fathers, who were led out of Egypt, out of bondage, and also were preserved in the wilderness by him, yea, the God of Abraham, and of Isaac, and the God of Jacob, yieldeth himself, according to the words of the angel, as a man, into the hands of wicked men, to be lifted up, according to the words of Zenock, and to be crucified, according to the words of Neum, and to be buried in a sepulchre, according to the words of Zenos, which he spake concerning the three days of darkness, which should be a sign given of his death unto those who should inhabit the isles of the sea, more especially given unto those who are of the house of Israel." (1 Ne. 19: 10).

> "And he said unto me that while the thunder and the lightning lasted, and the tempest, that these things should be, and that darkness should cover the face of the whole earth for the space of three days." Hel. 14: 27 (20, 27).

> "And it came to pass that thus did the three days pass away. And it was in the morning, and the darkness dispersed from off the face of the land, and the earth did cease to tremble, and the rocks did cease to rend, and the dreadful groanings did cease, and all the tumultuous noises did pass away" (3 Ne. 10: 9).

I once heard a very lengthy presentation that made the case that on this year there was an additional holiday on that same week which made both Friday and Saturday Sabbath Passover days. Therefore the crucifixion would have been on Thursday. I asked that question to a scriptural scholar and he made a very strong case that that was not the case. In reading in Talmage's Jesus the Christ here is what he says. Pg. 617-18

*"The day of the Passover Feast. Controversy has been rife for many centuries as to the day of the Passover feast in the week of our Lord's death. That He was crucified on Friday, the day before the Jewish Sabbath, and that He rose a resurrected Being on Sunday, the day following the Sabbath of the Jews, are facts attested by the four Gospel writers. From the three synoptists we infer that the last supper occurred on the evening of the first day of unleavened bread, and therefore at the beginning of the Jewish Friday. That the Lord's last supper was regarded by Himself and the apostles as a Passover meal appears from Matt. 26:2, 17, 18, 19 and parallel passages, Mark 14: 14-16: Luke 22:11-13; as also from Luke 22:7,15.*

*John, however, who wrote after the synoptists and who probably had their writings before him, as is indicated by the supplementary character of his testimony or "Gospel", intimates that the last supper of which Jesus and the Twelve partook together occurred before the Feast of the Passover (John 13:1,2); and the same writer informs us that on the following day, Friday, the Jews refrained from entering the Roman hall of judgment, lest they be defiled and so become unfit to eat the Passover (18:28). It should be remembered that by common usage the term "Passover" was applied not only to the day or season of the observance, but to the meal itself, and particularly to the slain lamb (Matt. 26:17; Mark 14:12, 14,16; Luke 22:8,11,13,15; John 18:28; compare 1 Cor. 5:7) John also specifies that the day of the crucifixion was "the preparation of the Passover" (19:14), and that the next day, which was Saturday, the Sabbath, "was an high day" (verse 31), that is a Sabbath rendered doubly sacred because of it being also a feast day.*

Talmage goes on to outline several of the points of view for the various cases for a Thursday crucifixion and a Friday crucifixion and after all my research I have put to rest this question by saying "it is of little importance to the central fact that our Savior was betrayed, crucified and rose triumphant on the great morning which we celebrate as Easter Sunday.

## The Evening of the Last Supper

As the week drew to a close, key events unfolded in sacred sequence.

Jesus was at the house of Simon the leper when a woman anointed His head with oil—an act He interpreted as preparation for His burial (Matthew 26:6-13).

On the morning of the first day of the Passover—likely Wednesday or Thursday—Jesus instructed His disciples to prepare the Passover meal. That evening, He sat down with the Twelve (Matthew 26:18–20). As they reclined at the table, He sorrowfully foretold His betrayal, prompting each disciple to ask, "Lord, is it I?" (Matthew 26:22).

In a profound act of humility, Jesus washed the disciples' feet, teaching that the greatest among them must be the servant of all (John 13:5–6).



See Ray L. Huntington and Camille Fronk, "Latter-day Clarity on Christ's Life and Teachings," Ensign, Jan. 1999, 28.

After the sacrament, Jesus delivered His final discourse to the Eleven, having excused Judas to carry out his betrayal. In this sacred moment, He taught the mission of the Holy Ghost, spoke of His coming death and resurrection, declared His divine Sonship, and offered the great Intercessory Prayer. He prayed for His apostles and all the faithful, declaring the unity of the Father and the Son (John 16–17).

They concluded by singing a hymn and walking to the Mount of Olives. There, Jesus again prophesied His death, warning that His disciples would scatter. Yet He also promised that after rising, He would go before them into Galilee. Peter objected, but Jesus foretold that Peter would deny Him three times before morning (Matthew 26:30–34).

They then entered Gethsemane. Leaving most of the disciples behind, Jesus took Peter, James, and John a little farther and asked them to watch. Three times He went further still to pray, and three times He returned to find them asleep (Matthew 26:36–45).

Much has been written—eloquently and reverently—about the suffering of our Savior in Gethsemane. Here, I simply express my deep appreciation and share His own words from modern revelation:

"Therefore I command you to repent... For behold, I, God, have suffered these things for all... Which suffering caused myself, even God, the greatest of all, to tremble because of pain, and to bleed at every pore... Nevertheless, glory be to the Father, and I partook and finished my preparations unto the children of men." (Doctrine and Covenants 19:15–19)

Like Nephi, who felt mighty in words yet weak in writing, I find myself weak in both when trying to express the grandeur of the Savior's sacrifice. I cannot fully articulate my gratitude. The only offering I can truly give is my life—my choices, my efforts to follow Him, my actions.

I've heard since childhood that Jesus suffered for each of our sins. I do not fully understand how that works, nor do I think it's simply transactional—that He suffered for my 2,345 sins and another's 4,398. I don't believe He suffered only for sins that would be repented of, or even every sin individually. Rather, I believe the law of justice is not a matter of tally marks and quotas.

Jesus Christ—perfect, divine, the literal Son of God—willingly took upon Himself unimaginable suffering. And because of who He is, all intelligences accepted Him as the Savior of mankind. His infinite sacrifice satisfied the demands of eternal justice not by accounting for each individual misstep, but by the completeness and purity of the offering itself. Only He, being perfect, universally loved, and eternally qualified, could both mete out mercy and justice with divine precision. And He will do so—perfectly.

I love Him for that.

I've often contemplated Alma 7:11–12 in the Book of Mormon. It beautifully teaches that Jesus Christ not only suffered for our sins, but also experienced our pains, sicknesses, and afflictions so He could know how to help us perfectly. Here's the passage:

> Alma 7:11–12 "And he shall go forth, suffering pains and
> afflictions and temptations of every kind; and this that the word
> might be fulfilled which saith he will take upon him the pains and
> the sicknesses of his people. And he will take upon him death,
> that he may loose the bands of death which bind his people;
> and he will take upon him their infirmities, that his bowels may
> be filled with mercy, according to the flesh, that he may know
> according to the flesh how to succor his people according to their
> infirmities."

This is one of the most tender and personal descriptions of the Savior's mission—showing that He didn't just die for us, He lived through every sorrow so He could understand us deeply and perfectly.

It was when He lived through everyone of my sorrows and my joys that His understanding was complete. How else could He ever know what it feels like to be stupid. Yes, He can know how we feel.

Now, back to His time in the Garden of Gethsemane.

We know very little about His prayer—only the beginning, recorded before the disciples fell asleep, if they are indeed the source. The New Testament tells us Christ was in agony, His soul "exceedingly sorrowful unto death" (Mark 14:34; see also Luke 22:44). But latter-day scripture opens a window into the depth, intensity, and scope of His suffering.

Christ took upon Himself "the pains of every living creature, both men, women, and children," that "the resurrection might pass upon all men" (2 Ne. 9:21–22). He suffered "even more than man can suffer," bleeding from every pore as He bore the anguish of mankind's sins (Mosiah 3:7; see also D&C 19:18; Luke 22:44). In one of the most sacred revelations ever recorded, the Savior told the Prophet Joseph:

> "Which suffering caused myself, even God, the greatest of all, to tremble because of pain, and to bleed at every pore, and to suffer both body and spirit—and would that I might not drink the bitter cup, and shrink— Nevertheless, glory be to the Father, and I partook and finished my preparations unto the children of men" (D&C 19:18–19; see also D&C 19:16–17; D&C 18:11).

Centuries before His birth, the descendants of Lehi knew how the Lord would die (1 Ne. 11:33; 1 Ne. 19:10; 2 Ne. 6:9; 2 Ne. 10:3–5). And after His death, their lands shook with earthquakes and were cloaked in three days of darkness, as Samuel the Lamanite had prophesied (Hel. 14:20–27; 3 Ne. 8:5–22; 3 Ne. 10:9). The absence of the "Light of the World" became painfully literal, even for those far from Jerusalem.

Christ Himself taught the symbolic significance of His Crucifixion:

> "My Father sent me that I might be lifted up upon the cross ... that I might draw all men unto me, that as I have been lifted up by men even so should men be lifted up by the Father ... to be judged of their works" (3 Ne. 27:14).

After Gethsemane, Judas arrived with the guards. Peter, in misguided zeal, cut off a soldier's ear, which Jesus immediately healed. Then began one of the most illegal trials in human history. For the detailed legal breakdown, I refer to Jesus the Christ, pp. 644–648, where Talmage outlines the grave violations of justice.

Now, a personal thought—I've always had a soft spot for Pilate. When Jesus said, "Father, forgive them, for they know not what they do," I believe He included the Roman soldiers—and Pilate.

I admire Pilate for two reasons.

**First, he was in an impossible position.** He had to balance the demands of a corrupt and apostate Jewish leadership with the political expectations from Rome. He wasn't a saint—he had political baggage the Jewish leaders could exploit. Yet, despite that pressure, he tried—repeatedly—to release Jesus. He recognized innocence and, I believe, glimpsed the truth. Had he been given the opportunity to fully hear and receive the Gospel under normal conditions, I believe he would have.

**Second, Pilate's decision—however reluctant—was necessary.** Without his decree, Jesus could not have given His life for us. The Atonement required the cross, and Pilate's reluctant role fulfilled prophecy.

I don't claim to understand exactly how the Atonement works. But I know—because the Spirit has witnessed it to me—that it does. And Pilate was part of that divine plan. I believe forgiveness reached even him. He didn't have the law, and as Christ Himself taught, those without knowledge are not held to the same standard (see John 15:22). That knowledge gives me hope—for Pilate, and for myself.

Following the trial, we know of the brutal beatings, the scourging, and finally, the horror of Roman crucifixion. But what leaves me speechless is this: the Savior, after taking on the pains of the world in Gethsemane, endured torture and still chose the moment of His death. He said, "It is finished," and then He gave up the ghost.

And I ask myself: how often do I, in my weakness, try to quit before the work is done? Shame on me.

# The Ninth Day of Christmas

*"I ascend unto my Father, and your Father;*
*and to my God, and your God."*

## The Resurrection of Jesus Christ

In all the accounts—ancient and modern—of the resurrection of our Savior, one verse still gives me goosebumps — His visit to Mary in the garden.

> "And when she had thus said, she turned herself back, and saw Jesus standing, and knew not that it was Jesus. Jesus saith unto her, Woman, why weepest thou? whom seekest thou? She, supposing him to be the gardener, saith unto him, Sir, if thou have borne him hence, tell me where thou hast laid him, and I will take him away. Jesus saith unto her, Mary. She turned herself, and saith unto him, Rabboni; which is to say, Master. Jesus saith unto her, Touch me not; for I am not yet ascended to my Father: but go to my brethren, and say unto them, I ascend unto my Father, and your Father; and to my God, and your God." (John 20:14–17)

This account moves me deeply—not just because Mary is heartbroken and overwhelmed with grief, but because the Savior responds with such tenderness. And what touches me most of all is this: He appeared to her even before He ascended to the Father. That sacred moment was so personal, so compassionate. It shows just how much He loved Mary—how much He knows and loves us individually.

I also find it profoundly beautiful that He spoke to Mary without immediately revealing Himself. And later, on the road to Emmaus, He walked and talked with two of His disciples, and they too did not recognize Him at first. I reflect on these moments and see them as expressions of what I might call the "human side" of His divine nature—His godhood cloaked in familiarity and humility. Is there such a thing? I believe there is.

And I pray that when He comes to me—whether in vision, whisper, or some unexpected form—I will recognize Him. That even if He comes in disguise, my heart will burn within me, and I will know it is Him. That I will know Him immediately.

I've always found it fascinating that when Alma the Prophet taught his son about the resurrection, he openly admitted he didn't know everything. He had studied it intensely, yes—but what he truly came to understand came through revelation.

> "Behold, he bringeth to pass the resurrection of the dead. But behold, my son, the resurrection is not yet. Now, I unfold unto you a mystery; nevertheless, there are many mysteries which are kept, that no one knoweth them save God himself. But I show unto you one thing which I have inquired diligently of God that I might know—that is concerning the resurrection." (Alma 40:3)

That line stands out to me: "I show unto you one thing which I have inquired diligently of God that I might know." There's a powerful lesson in that. If we want to understand something—even if it's a mystery—we must inquire diligently. Especially when it comes to eternal truths.

The resurrection is, without question, the central event in God's plan of salvation. Though we can't separate His death and resurrection—both are sacred and essential—I personally see the resurrection as the crowning day. The triumph. The grand exclamation point on the Atonement of Jesus Christ.

As much as I would love to dive into the mechanics of how the resurrection actually works—all the details and "cool ins and outs"—much of it has not yet been revealed. But I believe, as we grow in faith and readiness, more will be unfolded to us. Jacob taught:

"Behold, great and marvelous are the works of the Lord. How unsearchable are the depths of the mysteries of him; and it is impossible that man should find out all his ways. And no man knoweth of his ways save it be revealed unto him; wherefore, brethren, despise not the revelations of God." (Jacob 4:8)

So instead of speculating or creating my own theories, I'd rather review what the Lord has already revealed through His prophets—ancient and modern: Jesus, Peter, James, Paul, John, Nephi, Jacob, Lehi, Alma, Amulek, King Benjamin, Mosiah, Abinadi, Joseph Smith, Moses, Moroni, Gordon B. Hinckley, and Alma again.

Here's what they taught us about the resurrection:

- The resurrection is the uniting of the body and the spirit. (Alma 11:43–45; 40:18; 41:2–4; 42:23 – Alma and Amulek)

- After the resurrection, we can die no more. (Alma 11:45 – Amulek)

- A resurrected body is tangible. (3 Nephi 11:13–17 – Jesus Christ)

- It's a restoration, not a replacement. We will receive our same fundamental parts. (Alma 11:45; Mormon 6:21; History of the Church 5:339 – Joseph Smith)

- Everyone will be resurrected. Every person—without exception. Even translated beings will be resurrected. (Alma 11:41–44 – Testified by Lehi, Jacob, Abinadi, Samuel, Moroni, Alma, and Amulek)

- There is a time appointed for each of us to be resurrected. (Alma 40:8–10)

- Even animals will be resurrected. (D&C 29:23–25; D&C 77:2–3 – Joseph Smith)

- Resurrection is only possible through Jesus Christ. (Mosiah 16:7–8 – Abinadi)

- Resurrection began with Christ—this is known as the First Resurrection. (2 Nephi 2:8; 25:13; Mosiah 3:10 – Lehi, Mosiah, Benjamin)

- Little children are partakers in the First Resurrection. (Mosiah 15:24–25 – Abinadi)

- We will be resurrected to various degrees of glory. (1 Corinthians 15:39–44; D&C 88:21–24 – Paul, Joseph Smith)

- Resurrection is a central part of the Plan of Happiness. (Alma 41:2–11; 45:5, 8)

- Without resurrection, we would remain in misery forever. (2 Nephi 9:5–10 – Jacob)

- Without resurrection, there can be no joy. (2 Nephi 2:25 – Lehi)

- Happiness requires a body. (D&C 93:33–34; Teachings of the Prophet Joseph Smith, p. 181 – Joseph Smith)

- There is no salvation without a body.

- Resurrection is the greatest of all gifts. (Moses 7:62 – Enoch)

- Jesus was resurrected with a physical, immortal body of flesh and bones. The Doctrine and Covenants confirms: "The Father has a body of flesh and bones as tangible as man's; the Son also." (D&C 130:22; see also D&C 93:33; D&C 129:1–2)

The Prophet Brigham Young offered a profound insight into one of the mysteries surrounding the resurrection. He taught that the keys and ordinance of resurrection are not available to us in mortality:

*"We have not, neither can we receive here, the ordinance and
the keys of the resurrection. They will be given to those who have
passed off this stage of action and have received their bodies
again... They will be ordained, by those who hold the keys of the
resurrection, to go forth and resurrect the Saints, just as we receive
the ordinance of baptism, then the keys to baptize others for the
remission of sins. This is one of the ordinances we cannot receive
here, and there are many more." (Journal of Discourses 15:137)*

This sacred ordinance, according to Brigham Young, will be administered in the post-mortal realm, much like baptismal keys are administered in mortality.

Paul similarly testified that not all would be resurrected at once:

"But every man in his own order" (1 Corinthians 15:23).

Expounding upon this doctrine, Joseph Fielding Smith taught that the first resurrection is reserved for those who are worthy of the celestial kingdom and who will rise to meet the Savior at His Second Coming. Following closely will be those who lived honorable lives and kept a terrestrial law, along with those who died without a knowledge of the gospel but would have received it with their whole hearts. These all participate in the first resurrection.

By contrast, the second resurrection, also referred to as the resurrection of the unjust, will not occur until after the Millennium. It will include the rest of mankind—those who lived wickedly and unrepentantly: "liars, and sorcerers, and adulterers, and all who love and make a lie." These will inherit the telestial kingdom or become sons of perdition (see Doctrines of Salvation, 2:297).

Even Alma acknowledged that the timing and order of the resurrection was not fully revealed to him. He pondered whether there might be multiple appointed times for resurrection:

"Now, whether there shall be one time, or a second time, or a
third time, that men shall come forth from the dead, it mattereth
not; for God knoweth all these things; and it sufficeth me to know
that this is the case—that there is a time appointed that all shall
rise from the dead." (Alma 40:5)

Alma went on to share his opinion that those who had died before the resurrection of Christ would rise before those who died afterward (Alma 40:19). President Joseph Fielding Smith later clarified that this view was based on Alma's limited understanding at the time:

*"It is evident that Alma's understanding of the extent of the
resurrection at the time the Savior came forth from the dead was
limited, therefore he stated only his opinion." (Charles D. Tate and*

Monte S. Lyman, *Alma: The Testimony of the Word*, p. 495)

Nevertheless, Alma correctly affirmed that only the righteous would rise with Christ in the resurrection (Alma 40:20–21). This stood in contrast to his strong and sure testimony regarding the spirit world, which had been revealed to him directly by an angel (Alma 40:11–14).

Before Alma, the prophet Abinadi had clearly taught that the resurrection of the righteous and those who died without a knowledge of the gospel would begin with the resurrection of Christ and continue through the end of the Millennium. He was firm in stating that the wicked would have no part in the first resurrection:

> "And these are those who have part in the first resurrection;
> and these are they that have died before Christ came, in their
> ignorance, not having salvation declared unto them. And thus the
> Lord bringeth about the restoration of these; and they have a part
> in the first resurrection, or have eternal life, being redeemed by
> the Lord." (Mosiah 15:22–26)

A foundational truth in all of this is that the resurrection could not begin until Christ had completed His mortal mission, atoned for our sins, and obtained the keys of resurrection. Only after His triumph over death could the ordinances of salvation for the dead—baptism, sealing, ordination—begin to be performed.

President Joseph Fielding Smith clarified this critical point when asked whether vicarious ordinances such as baptisms or anointings were performed in the Temple of Solomon. He replied:

> *"There is nothing recorded in the Old Testament declaring that
> gospel ordinances were performed in the Temple of Solomon in
> the interest of the dead. It appears very clear... that nothing in any
> manner conveys the thought that vicarious work was performed in
> those early times for the dead. Until the Son of God had finished
> his preparations for the salvation of man and to bring to pass the
> resurrection of the dead, there could be no ordinance or labor
> of any kind pertaining to the resurrection and redemption of
> mankind that could be performed for the dead. Therefore, in the
> Temple of Solomon the ordinances were evidently confined to the
> living." (Answers to Gospel Questions, Vol. 2, p. 164)*

The resurrection stands as a divine gift—one that began with the Savior, continues with the righteous, and will reach every soul according to God's perfect timing and order.

Immediately following His resurrection, the Savior made a profound declaration to His disciples:

"All power is given unto me in heaven and in earth. Go ye therefore, and teach all nations, baptizing them in the name of the Father, and of the Son, and of the Holy Ghost" (Matthew 28:18–19).

This statement implies that prior to His resurrection, Jesus had not yet received all power in heaven and on earth. It was only after overcoming death that He was fully invested with divine authority. From that point forward, His disciples were commissioned to preach His gospel to every nation and to perform sacred ordinances—first for the living, and eventually for the dead. The scope of His authority now extended beyond the living to encompass all mankind, across all dispensations.

Abinadi, teaching the rebellious Nephites, spoke prophetically of the necessity and power of Christ's resurrection:

"The time shall come when all shall see the salvation of the Lord; when every nation, kindred, tongue, and people shall confess before God that his judgments are just. And now if Christ had not come into the world, speaking of things to come as though they had already come, there could have been no redemption. And if Christ had not risen from the dead, or have broken the bands of death that the grave should have no victory, and that death should have no sting, there could have been no resurrection. But there is a resurrection, therefore the grave hath no victory, and the sting of death is swallowed up in Christ. He is the light and the life of the world; yea, a light that is endless, that can never be darkened; yea, and also a life which is endless, that there can be no more death." (Mosiah 16:1, 6–9)

Building on Brigham Young's earlier teachings, we begin to understand that resurrection is not only a miracle, but a priesthood ordinance—one that has not yet been revealed in full to mortal men. Elder Critchlow observed in the April 1963 General Conference that resurrection is indeed a function of priesthood power:

*"May I ask—how can we achieve eternal life without the blessings and ordinances of the priesthood?"*

Robert J. Matthews, in his presentation "Behold the Messiah," expounded upon the Apostle Paul's insights in 1 Corinthians 15, where Paul posed two fundamental questions about the resurrection: "How are the dead raised up? and with what body do they come?" (1 Cor. 15:35). Paul answers that although all will be raised, not all will receive the same glory (vv. 29–42), yet all will receive an incorruptible, immortal body (vv. 42–44). He teaches that this resurrected body is the same "natural body" the spirit occupied during mortality, now glorified and perfected (see also D&C 88:28).

Modern prophets and apostles have clarified that the resurrection will proceed in an orderly and priesthood-directed manner. Just as one cannot baptize others without first receiving baptism and ordination, so too one cannot resurrect another until they themselves have been resurrected and given the keys of that ordinance.

Brigham Young and Elder Erastus Snow taught in the Journal of Discourses that the resurrection will occur under priesthood authority through delegation. President Young even stated that the Prophet Joseph Smith will be the first to be resurrected in this dispensation and will be given the keys to begin the work, enabling others to be resurrected in order.

In the April 1977 General Conference, President Spencer W. Kimball quoted Brigham Young:

> *"We are in possession of all the ordinances that can be administered in the flesh; but there are other ordinances and administrations that must be administered beyond this world. I know you would like to ask what they are. I will mention one. We have not, neither can we receive here, the ordinance and the keys of resurrection."* (Conference Report, April 1977, p. 69)

This sacred act, so essential to salvation, is governed by the Melchizedek Priesthood and is also part of the patriarchal order of the eternal family. In this framework, the resurrection becomes a family-centered ordinance, carried out by resurrected beings with authority, possibly beginning with righteous patriarchs who call forth their own posterity.

This perspective leads us to consider whether even Jesus raised Himself, or whether He, too, was resurrected by divine priesthood authority. Peter's testimony in Acts suggests the latter:

- "God hath raised [Jesus] up" (Acts 2:24)

- "This Jesus hath God raised up" (Acts 2:32)

- "The God of our fathers raised up Jesus" (Acts 5:30)

If these verses are read literally and taken together with the teachings of President Young and Elder Snow, we may understand the resurrection not as a spontaneous self-action, but as a divine priesthood act performed by one with authority, possibly within the eternal order of families.

John offers a curious detail in his account of the empty tomb:

> "The napkin, that was about his head, not lying with the linen clothes, but wrapped together in a place by itself" (John 20:7).

This deliberate act of folding the burial clothes seems to suggest that Jesus' emergence from the grave was dignified, deliberate, and divinely directed.

Matthew testifies that after Christ's resurrection:

> "Many bodies of the saints which slept arose, and came out of
> the graves after his resurrection, and went into the holy city, and
> appeared unto many" (Matt. 27:52–53).

Likewise, in the Western Hemisphere, following His visit to the Nephites, the Savior confirmed that others had also been resurrected and appeared to His people (3 Nephi 23:9–13).

Together, these teachings weave a beautiful tapestry of understanding: that resurrection is not only real but holy, governed by divine order and priesthood power, and ultimately part of the eternal plan by which families may live forever.

## The Resurrection: A Divine Necessity and a Testimony of Jesus Christ's Power

Resurrection is not just a profound doctrine—it is a divine necessity, made so by the Fall of Adam. Because of Adam's transgression, physical death became the universal lot of all mankind. Therefore, as Paul so clearly teaches, "as in Adam all die, even so in Christ shall all be made alive" (1 Corinthians 15:22). The Book of Mormon, with prophetic clarity, outlines the law governing resurrection. Alma declares:

> "The spirit and the body shall be reunited again in its perfect
> form; both limb and joint shall be restored to its proper frame...
> this restoration shall come to all, both old and young, both bond
> and free, both male and female... and even there shall not so
> much as a hair of their heads be lost; but everything shall be
> restored to its perfect frame" (Alma 11:42–44).

This resurrection is complete and absolute: not one part of the body will be missing, and the union of body and spirit will never again be broken. "The spirit and the body is restored to itself again, and all men become incorruptible, and immortal... and they can die no more" (Alma 11:45). These eternal principles affirm that once resurrected, a person is beyond the reach of physical death forever.

Such firm declarations invite us to reflect more deeply on the scope of the Savior's role in the eternal plan. One often-asked question is: "Is Jesus the Redeemer of other worlds besides our own?" The answer, taught plainly in scripture, is "Yes." The Lord revealed to the Prophet Joseph Smith that "by him, and through him, and of him, the worlds are and were created, and the inhabitants thereof are begotten sons and daughters unto God" (D&C 76:24; see also D&C 88:51–61).

Then follows the next question: "Did Jesus suffer and die on other worlds for the sins of those other worlds as He did for ours?" Here the scriptures speak again. According to Alma 11 and its revealed truths, we must answer "No." The Atonement of Jesus Christ—the agony in Gethsemane, the death on the cross, and the rising from the tomb—were singular events, never to be repeated. Had He suffered and died on any other world, He could not have done so again here. The eternal record affirms that these infinite acts happened once, on this earth, never to be duplicated. This is the uniqueness of our planet in the cosmos—it is the chosen footstool of the Almighty (D&C 38:17), the place where Christ took upon Himself a mortal body, where He overcame death, and where He will return in the flesh to reign eternally (D&C 130:9).

## Jesus Christ and the Power Over Death

Because all mankind is subject to the two deaths introduced by the Fall—spiritual and physical—how then was Jesus able to overcome death when no other mortal could? The Apostle Paul gives a beautiful insight when he says that Jesus "led captivity captive" (Ephesians 4:8). Death, which had enslaved all humanity, was itself overcome by the very Son of God.

Jesus had power over death because of His unique divine parentage. As Nephi testified, He was "the Son of God in the flesh" (1 Nephi 11:18, 21). Helaman echoes this truth: "It is by him that salvation cometh. Therefore he is the light and the life of the world; yea, a light that is endless, that can never be darkened… and also a life which is endless, that there can be no more death" (Helaman 5:11). Mormon affirms the same in his writings (Mormon 7:5–6).

The life of Jesus Christ was not simply the life of a man—it was the life of a God. Alma explains that Christ's sacrifice "was not a human sacrifice; but it must be an infinite and eternal sacrifice" (Alma 34:10). Jesus inherited life from His Father—divine life, with divine power over death. He declared this Himself:

> "For as the Father hath life in himself; so hath he given to the Son to have life in himself" (John 5:26).

He also testified:

> "Therefore doth my Father love me, because I lay down my life, that I might take it again. No man taketh it from me, but I lay it down of myself. I have power to lay it down, and I have power to take it again" (John 10:17–18).

What a wondrous doctrine this is! The Savior was not a passive victim of death; He was its Master. Death had no claim on Him. His life was not taken—it was given. And because He lives again, we too shall live.

If Jesus had been subject to death in the same way all of us are—if death had come for Him as a natural and inescapable end—then His offering might be seen merely as a surrender of time. But this was not so. Jesus Christ was not under the bondage of death. Because He did not have to die, His choice to lay down His life was the fullest, most complete gift that could ever be given. He didn't just give His time—He gave His life, voluntarily and entirely, to pay the infinite price of sin. That distinction is essential. He chose death, and therefore His sacrifice is infinitely more profound.

It may have been this unique power over death that allowed Jesus to refer to those who had died as merely being "asleep." When He came to the house of Jairus and found that the twelve-year-old girl had died, He told those gathered, "The damsel is not dead, but sleepeth." (Mark 5:39). They laughed Him to scorn, knowing she was dead. But Jesus, who held complete dominion over death, restored her life, and in doing so taught something far deeper than they realized. To Him, death is not the end—it is temporary, like sleep.

He spoke the same way of Lazarus, who had lain in the tomb for four days. Jesus told His disciples, "Our friend Lazarus sleepeth; but I go, that I may awake him out of sleep." (John 11:11). Without the light of the gospel, death seems final—an unyielding separation. But Jesus was always the teacher, always leading us to see the eternal. By calling death "sleep," He was preparing our minds to understand resurrection—that death is not the end, but a passing pause.

This language served as more than a metaphor; it was an attention-getter, a way to teach profound doctrine in a simple phrase. Death is not final. In the hands of the Savior, it is but a slumber from which He can awaken any soul.

After His resurrection, Jesus remained on the earth for forty days, visiting with the Apostles and preparing them for their ministry. He then ascended to heaven from the Mount of Olives, near Bethany (Acts 1:9–12; Luke 24:50–52). As He rose, two angels appeared and testified to the eleven disciples, declaring that "this same Jesus" would return one day. That witness matters. It means that the same resurrected Jesus—who ascended in a glorified body of flesh and bone—will return in that same body. He is not an idea or a symbol. He is real, and He will come again as He left.

I am grateful for Robert J. Matthews and others who have given voice to these truths with such clarity, from whom I have taken much of this. Their words echo the testimony in my own heart. The Savior lives. He conquered death not only for Himself, but for all of us. And He will return—in that same body He bore on the cross, the same body He showed to Thomas, and the same body He took with Him into heaven.

There is no shortage of witnesses to the sacred reality that our Savior, Jesus Christ, is a resurrected being. The scriptures offer powerful and compelling testimonies of those who saw Him, spoke with Him, and bore record of His living presence after His crucifixion and resurrection.

The Prophet Joseph Smith declared, in perhaps the most direct and stirring testimony recorded in this dispensation:

> "And now, after the many testimonies which have been given of him, this is the testimony, last of all, which we give of him: That he lives! For we saw him, even on the right hand of God; and we heard the voice bearing record that he is the Only Begotten of the Father— That by him, and through him, and of him, the worlds are and were created, and the inhabitants thereof are begotten sons and daughters unto God." (Doctrine and Covenants 76:22–24)

This testimony affirms not only the living reality of Christ but His eternal role in creation and salvation.

The New Testament provides a detailed record of the many appearances Jesus made following His resurrection—each a sacred witness that He had indeed risen with a glorified body of flesh and bone. Consider this chronological list of those sacred visitations:

- To Mary Magdalene — On the morning of the resurrection, Jesus appeared first to Mary (Mark 16:9–10; John 20:1–18). She was the first witness of His resurrection.

- To the other women — That same morning, other faithful women saw Him and held Him by the feet, worshiping Him (Matthew 28:9–10).

- To two disciples on the road to Emmaus — That afternoon, Jesus walked and conversed with two disciples, opening their understanding to the scriptures (Mark 16:12–13; Luke 24:13–32).

- To Peter — Later that day, the Lord appeared to Peter (Luke 24:34).

- To ten Apostles — That evening, Jesus appeared to the Apostles in a closed room—Thomas being absent. He showed them His hands and feet and ate fish and honeycomb in their presence to demonstrate He was not a spirit but resurrected in the flesh (Mark 16:14; Luke 24:36–40; John 20:19–25).

- To the eleven, including Thomas — One week later, Jesus appeared again. This time, Thomas was present and invited to touch the nail prints in the Savior's hands and feet and to thrust his hand into His side (John 20:26–31).

- To seven disciples by the Sea of Galilee — Jesus appeared to them while they were fishing. He dined with them and taught them again (John 21).

• To the Eleven and over five hundred others — On a mountain in Galilee, Jesus gave His great commission (Matthew 28:16–20; 1 Corinthians 15:6).

• To James — The Lord also appeared to His half-brother James, though the time and place are not specified (1 Corinthians 15:7).

• To the Eleven on the day of His Ascension — Near Bethany, Jesus was taken up into heaven while blessing them (Mark 16:19; Luke 24:44–51; Acts 1:3).

• To Paul — Years later, Jesus appeared to Saul (later Paul) on the road to Damascus, changing the course of Paul's life and ministry (Acts 9:1–9; Acts 22:6; 1 Corinthians 9:1; 1 Corinthians 15:8).

• To John the Revelator — In approximately A.D. 96, the Savior appeared in glory to John on the Isle of Patmos and declared, "I am he that liveth, and was dead; and, behold, I am alive for evermore" (Revelation 1:9–18).

These appearances are not exhaustive. As Acts 1:3 states, Jesus "showed himself alive after his passion by many infallible proofs, being seen of them forty days, and speaking of the things pertaining to the kingdom of God." Additionally, Acts 10:41 and Acts 13:31 affirm that He appeared "not to all the people, but unto witnesses chosen before of God," suggesting that many sacred visitations occurred that were not recorded in detail.

These witnesses—both ancient and modern—stand as eternal declarations that Jesus of Nazareth lives. He rose from the grave, conquered death, and continues to minister in glory. This knowledge is at the heart of the restored gospel and the foundation of my faith.

# The Tenth Day of Christmas



*"Behold my Beloved Son,"*

## Christ's Appearance to Nephites on the American Continent

Consider the immense time and effort dedicated to guiding figures like Lehi, Nephi, Sariah, Jacob, Benjamin, Alma, Helaman, and Mormon. These and dozens of others tirelessly bore witness to the people, testifying of Christ's divinity. Consider the size of a list of all the prophecies foretelling Christ's birth, death, and eventual appearance in the Americas. Despite the miracles, the parables, the examples, the prayers along with the wickedness, rejection, and crucifixion in Jerusalem, Christ left behind only a small group of faithful believers. Now, in His glory, He comes—not as a glory-seeker, remember how He always gave full credit to His Father. Now, Heavenly Father Himself introduces Jesus Christ, declaring, "In whom I am well pleased, in whom I have glorified my name." Christ appeared to a welcoming crowd, a home crowd, not to destroy, but to teach, love, and bless. No Sadducees, Pharisees, or Romans here—just believers. What a sweet day that would have been!

Here is the record right out of the Book of Mormon.

1 AND now it came to pass that there were a great multitude gathered together, of the people of Nephi, round about the temple which was in the land Bountiful; and they were marveling and wondering one with another, and were showing one to another the great and marvelous change which had taken place.

2 And they were also conversing about this Jesus Christ, of whom the sign had been given concerning his death.

3 And it came to pass that while they were thus conversing one with another, they heard a voice as if it came out of heaven; and they cast their eyes round about, for they understood not the voice which they heard; and it was not a harsh voice, neither was it a loud voice; nevertheless, and notwithstanding it being a small

voice it did pierce them that did hear to the center, insomuch that there was no part of their frame that it did not cause to quake; yea, it did pierce them to the very soul, and did cause their hearts to burn.

4 And it came to pass that again they heard the voice, and they understood it not.

5 And again the third time they did hear the voice, and did open their ears to hear it; and their eyes were towards the sound thereof; and they did look steadfastly towards heaven, from whence the sound came.

6 And behold, the third time they did understand the voice which they heard; and it said unto them:

7 Behold my Beloved Son, in whom I am well pleased, in whom I have glorified my name—hear ye him.

8 And it came to pass, as they understood they cast their eyes up again towards heaven; and behold, they saw a Man descending out of heaven; and he was clothed in a white robe; and he came down and stood in the midst of them; and the eyes of the whole multitude were turned upon him, and they durst not open their mouths, even one to another, and wist not what it meant, for they thought it was an angel that had appeared unto them.

9 And it came to pass that he stretched forth his hand and spake unto the people, saying:

10 Behold, I am Jesus Christ, whom the prophets testified shall come into the world.

11 And behold, I am the light and the life of the world; and I have drunk out of that bitter cup which the Father hath given me, and have glorified the Father in taking upon me the sins of the world, in the which I have suffered the will of the Father in all things from the beginning.

12 And it came to pass that when Jesus had spoken these words the whole multitude fell to the earth; for they remembered that it had been prophesied among them that Christ should show himself unto them after his ascension into heaven.

13 And it came to pass that the Lord spake unto them saying:

14 Arise and come forth unto me, that ye may thrust your hands into my side, and also that ye may feel the prints of the nails in my hands and in my feet, that ye may know that I am the God of

Israel, and the God of the whole earth, and have been slain for the sins of the world.

15 And it came to pass that the multitude went forth, and thrust their hands into his side, and did feel the prints of the nails in his hands and in his feet; and this they did do, going forth one by one until they had all gone forth, and did see with their eyes and did feel with their hands, and did know of a surety and did bear record, that it was he, of whom it was written by the prophets, that should come.

16 And when they had all gone forth and had witnessed for themselves, they did cry out with one accord, saying:

17 Hosanna! Blessed be the name of the Most High God! And they did fall down at the feet of Jesus, and did worship him.

I would also fall down to His feet and worship!

Jesus taught the same Gospel in the Americas as He did in the Old World, but two aspects of His ministry here stand out to me: His emphasis on recording Samuel's testimony and His teachings on prayer.

First, Jesus instructs the people to study the scriptures and requests to review the records kept by the prophets. This moment is significant.

This is in 3 Nephi 23.

> 1 AND now, behold, I say unto you, that ye ought to search these things. Yea, a commandment I give unto you that ye search these things diligently; for great are the words of Isaiah.
>
> 2 For surely he spake as touching all things concerning my people which are of the house of Israel; therefore it must needs be that he must speak also to the Gentiles.
>
> 3 And all things that he spake have been and shall be, even according to the words which he spake.
>
> 4 Therefore give heed to my words; write the things which I have told you; and according to the time and the will of the Father they shall go forth unto the Gentiles.
>
> 5 And whosoever will hearken unto my words and repenteth and is baptized, the same shall be saved. Search the prophets, for many there be that testify of these things.
>
> 6 And now it came to pass that when Jesus had said these words he said unto them again, after he had expounded all the scriptures unto them which they had received, he said unto them:

Behold, other scriptures I would that ye should write, that ye have not.

7 And it came to pass that he said unto Nephi: Bring forth the record which ye have kept.

8 And when Nephi had brought forth the records, and laid them before him, he cast his eyes upon them and said:

9 Verily I say unto you, I commanded my servant Samuel, the Lamanite, that he should testify unto this people, that at the day that the Father should glorify his name in me that there were many saints who should arise from the dead, and should appear unto many, and should minister unto them. And he said unto them: Was it not so?

10 And his disciples answered him and said: Yea, Lord, Samuel did prophesy according to thy words, and they were all fulfilled.

11 And Jesus said unto them: How be it that ye have not written this thing, that many saints did arise and appear unto many and did minister unto them?

12 And it came to pass that Nephi remembered that this thing had not been written.

13 And it came to pass that Jesus commanded that it should be written; therefore it was written according as he commanded.

14 And now it came to pass that when Jesus had expounded all the scriptures in one, which they had written, he commanded them that they should teach the things which he had expounded unto them.

I'm just fascinated by how Jesus revealed truths to Samuel and commanded him to teach, only to show up years later—He, the very source of those teachings—quoting the prophets He inspired. His message never wavers; it's the heart of His mission to exalt us. If the Savior can teach from His own prophets, so can we!

Second, Another thing that always strikes me is the emphasis on prayer. I don't recall the New Testament hitting me with such a powerful sense of how sacred prayer is. Sure, Jesus taught it and prayed constantly, but just look at how one of those prayers is described here. It's incredible!

This prayer is found in 3 Nephi 17.

15 "And when he had said these words, he himself also knelt upon the earth; and behold he prayed unto the Father, and the

things which he prayed cannot be written, and the multitude did bear record who heard him. 16 And after this manner do they bear record: The eye hath never seen, neither hath the ear heard, before, so great and marvelous things as we saw and heard Jesus speak unto the Father;

17 And no tongue can speak, neither can there be written by any man, neither can the hearts of men conceive so great and marvelous things as we both saw and heard Jesus speak; and no one can conceive of the joy which filled our souls at the time we heard him pray for us unto the Father.

18 And it came to pass that when Jesus had made an end of praying unto the Father, he arose; but so great was the joy of the multitude that they were overcome." (3 Nephi 17:15-18)

We have been given so much. We have a living prophet, conference twice a year, and more scriptures than any people at any time in history, and yet I can't wait to hear a prayer like the one described in verse 17.

A few friends and I were discussing some of the mysteries that interested us. One asked, "When you meet the Savior, what are you going to ask?" The various questions proposed included topics about dinosaurs, crazy historical events, and some current cultural challenges. I said, "I will ask Jesus to kneel with me and pray to His and my Father in Heaven because I want to hear a prayer that no tongue can speak, neither can be written by any man, nor can the hearts of men conceive such great and marvelous things. And I want to experience the joy that no one can conceive. I want to be overcome."

When I conceive of my lack of conception, my mind goes mushy. It scares me to death that I go around thinking I have a handle on things. I realize that I know so little and want to know so much. It must make my Heavenly Father laugh at His little son down here who is such a dope. It is a good thing that I know He loves me.

Once the Savior was finished teaching here in America, I imagine a similar event happened somewhere else, possibly multiple times. These were wonderful days for our Savior.

# THE ELEVENTH DAY OF CHRISTMAS

*"This is My Beloved Son. Hear Him!"*

## Christ's Appearance to Joseph Smith in 1820

I can't describe this sacred event more beautifully than President Gordon B. Hinckley did in October 2007 General Conference.

> "When Jesus walked the earth, He said, "This is life eternal, that they might know thee the only true God, and Jesus Christ, whom thou hast sent" (John 17:3).

Joseph, when he was 14 years of age, had an experience in that glorious First Vision that was different from any other recorded experience of any man. At no other time of which we have any record have God, our Eternal Father, and His Beloved Son, the risen Lord, appeared on earth together.

At the time of the baptism of Jesus by John in the river Jordan, the voice of God was heard, but He was not seen. At the Mount of Transfiguration, again the voice of God was heard, but there is no record of His appearance. Stephen saw the Lord on the right hand of the Father, but They did not address or instruct him.

Following His Resurrection, Jesus appeared to the Nephites in the Western Hemisphere. The voice of the Almighty was heard three times, introducing the risen Christ, but there was no appearance of the Father.

How truly remarkable was that vision in the year 1820 when Joseph prayed in the woods and there appeared before him both the Father and the Son. One of these spoke to him, calling him by name and, pointing to the other, said, "This is My Beloved Son. Hear Him!" (Joseph Smith—History 1:17).

Nothing like it had ever happened before. One is led to wonder why it was so important that both the Father and the Son appear. I think it was because They were ushering in the dispensation of the fulness of times, the last and final dispensation of the gospel, when there would be gathered together in one the elements of all previous dispensations. This was to be the final chapter in the long chronicle of God's dealing with men and women upon the earth.

Following the Savior's death, the Church He had established drifted into apostasy. Fulfilled were the words of Isaiah, who said, "The earth also is defiled under the inhabitants thereof; because they have transgressed the laws, changed the ordinance, broken the everlasting covenant" (Isaiah 24:5).

Realizing the importance of knowing the true nature of God, men had struggled to find a way to define Him. Learned clerics argued with one another. When Constantine became a Christian in the fourth century, he called together a great convocation of learned men with the hope that they could reach a conclusion of understanding concerning the true nature of Deity. All they reached was a compromise of various points of view. The result was the Nicene Creed of a.d. 325. This and subsequent creeds have become the declaration of doctrine concerning the nature of Deity for most of Christianity ever since.

I have read them all a number of times. I cannot understand them. I think others cannot understand them. I am sure that the Lord also knew that many would not understand them. And so in 1820, in that incomparable vision, the Father and the Son appeared to the boy Joseph. They spoke to him with words that were audible, and he spoke to Them. They could see. They could speak. They could hear. They were personal. They were of substance. They were not imaginary beings. They were beings tabernacled in flesh. And out of that experience has come our unique and true understanding of the nature of Deity.

No wonder that when Joseph in 1842 wrote the Articles of Faith, he stated as number one, "We believe in God, the Eternal Father, and in His Son, Jesus Christ, and in the Holy Ghost" (Articles of Faith 1:1)."

I hope you can clearly see why this was a special day for our Savior. He and His Father, together in Majesty, come to earth and begin the restoration of Their work and glory.

This moment, prepared for millennia, fulfilled ancient prophecies. Studying the apostasy and restoration with our youth, we compiled "Top Ten" lists to outline these events. Here they are, with a brief phrase explaining each entry's significance.

## Top Ten Top Tens of the Apostasy and Restoration

### Top Ten Prophecies of the Apostasy

- 2 Timothy 3:1-6 – Predicts perilous times and apostasy. Foretells spiritual decline.

- 2 Timothy 4:1-4 – People reject sound doctrine. Warns of false teachings.

- 1 Timothy 4:1 – Many depart from the faith. Signals widespread apostasy.

- Acts 20:29-30 – Grievous wolves enter the flock. Alerts to internal corruption.

- Revelation 13:4, 6-9 – Satan overcomes saints. Describes spiritual warfare.

- Jude 17-18 – Mockers arise in the last days. Highlights end-time skepticism.

- 2 Peter 2:1-3 – False teachers deceive many. Exposes doctrinal betrayal.

- 2 Thessalonians 2:3-4 – A falling away precedes Christ's return. Marks apostasy's timeline.

- Matthew 24:4-6 – Deceivers mislead the faithful. Urges vigilance.

- Isaiah 24:1-5 – Earth defiled by broken covenants. Links sin to spiritual decay.

## Top Ten Internal Causes of the Apostasy

- Pride – Fueled self-righteousness. Blinds to truth.

- Greed – Corrupted motives. Undermines charity.

- Disobedience – Ignored God's laws. Breaks covenants.

- Clinging to Law of Moses – Resisted new revelation. Stifles progress.

- Doctrinal corruption – Twisted Christ's teachings. Confuses believers.

- Contention – Divided the Church. Destroys unity.

- Ignorance – Spirit withdrew. Darkens understanding.

- Rebellion – Defied authority. Rejects God's order.

- Unauthorized rituals – Altered sacred ordinances. Invalidates covenants.

- Organizational changes – Disrupted priesthood structure. Weakens authority.

## Top Ten External Causes of Apostasy

- Persecution – Crushed faithful. Tests resolve.

- Loss of leadership – Left Church directionless. Creates vulnerability.

- Foreign doctrines – Infiltrated truth. Dilutes gospel.

- Indifference to learning – Stagnated growth. Limits revelation.

- Loss of worship rights – Restricted practice. Hinders faith.

- Tyranny over souls – Controlled beliefs. Stifles freedom.

- Spirit's withdrawal – Abandoned the wicked. Darkens hearts.

- No personal scriptures – Limited access to truth. Starves souls.

- Poor communication – Isolated believers. Breaks community.

- Political conflicts – Destabilized Church. Disrupts stability.

## Top Ten Persecutions of the Early Church

- Jews – Opposed Christian rise. Sparked early trials.

- Nero – Brutally targeted Christians. Ignited martyrdom.

- Domitian – Demanded emperor worship. Forced loyalty tests.

- Trajan – Formalized persecutions. Legalized oppression.

- Marcus Aurelius – Philosophized against faith. Justified cruelty.

- Severus – Banned conversions. Stifled growth.

- Maximinus – Renewed violent purges. Terrorized believers.

- Decius Trajan – Demanded sacrifices. Enforced apostasy.

- Diocletian – Launched Great Persecution. Aimed to eradicate.

- Inquisition – Later crushed dissent. Prolonged suffering.

## Top Ten Corruptions of Christ's Doctrines

- Nature of God – Misdefined Deity. Obscures truth.

- Godhead – Blurred distinct roles. Confuses identity.

- Predestination – Denied agency. Limits accountability.

- Indulgences – Sold salvation. Corrupts repentance.

- Spiritual gifts – Rejected miracles. Denies power.

- Revelation – Closed heavens. Silences God.

- Faith vs. works – Misbalanced salvation. Skews effort.

- No absolute truth – Embraced relativism. Undermines certainty.

- Purpose of body – Devalued physicality. Misaligns eternity.

- Tithing – Abused sacred funds. Exploits devotion.

## Top Ten Ordinances Lost or Perverted

- Sacrament – Altered symbolism. Weakens remembrance.

- Baptism by immersion – Replaced with sprinkling. Invalidates form.

- Gift of Holy Ghost – Ignored confirmation. Neglects guidance.

- Priesthood authority – Lost through apostasy. Breaks succession.

- Baptisms for dead – Abandoned proxy work. Limits salvation.

- Temple work – Forsaken sacred rites. Forfeits eternity.

- Infant baptism – Misapplied ordinance. Ignores agency.

- Church organization – Corrupted structure. Disrupts order.

- Marriage – Enforced celibacy. Defies divine plan.

- Resurrection – Questioned physical reality. Doubts victory.

## Top Ten Prophecies of the Restoration

- Revelation 14:6-8 – Angel restores gospel. Heralds truth.

- Matthew 24:14 – Gospel preached worldwide. Fulfills reach.

- Daniel 2:44-45 – Unstoppable kingdom rises. Establishes Zion.

- Daniel 7:27 – Saints inherit kingdom. Promises victory.

- Isaiah 2:2 – Temple in mountains. Centers worship.

- Isaiah 11:11 – God recovers remnant. Gathers Israel.

- Isaiah 29:14 – Marvelous work unfolds. Restores truth.

- Malachi 3:1 – Messenger prepares way. Clears path.

- Acts 3:21 – Restitution of all things. Renews gospel.

- Romans 11:25 – Gentiles receive fulness. Expands reach.

## Top Ten Geo/Political Changes for Restoration

- Columbus' voyage – Opened Americas. Set stage.

- Revolutionary War – Freed nation. Secured liberty.

- Maritime trade – Connected world. Spread ideas.

- Constitution – Protected rights. Enabled worship.

- Pilgrims – Sought religious freedom. Planted seeds.

- Crusades – Sparked learning. Ignited knowledge.

- Explorers – Expanded horizons. Bridged cultures.

- Education – Empowered masses. Fostered inquiry.

- King George's errors – Fueled independence. Broke tyranny.

- Reformation – Challenged dogma. Paved way.

## Top Ten Reformers

- John Wycliffe – Translated Bible into English. Empowered laity.

- Ulrich Zwingli – Simplified Swiss worship. Challenged rituals.

- John Calvin – Shaped Protestant theology. Defined grace.

- Martin Luther – Nailed 95 Theses. Sparked Reformation.

- William Tyndale - Translated the Bible from the original Greek and Hebrew - Much of the King James Bible is William Tyndale's - In my opinion all the beautiful words are his.

- John Wesley – Founded Methodism. Revived piety.

- Philipp Melanchthon – Systematized Lutheran doctrine. Clarified beliefs.

- John Knox – Reformed Scottish Church. Strengthened Presbyterianism.

- Roger Williams – Championed religious liberty. Defended freedom.

- Jerome of Prague – Preached reform early. Inspired change.

## Top Ten Technological Advances Required to Usher In and Maintain Restoration

- Printing Press – Mass-produced scriptures. Spreads truth.

- Paper – Enabled affordable books. Democratizes knowledge.

- Gunpowder – Shifted warfare, stabilized regions. Secures peace.

- Mariner Compass – Guided exploration. Connects continents.

- Movable Type – Streamlined printing. Accelerates literacy.

- Electricity – Powered modern tools. Drives progress.

- Telephones – Linked distant voices. Unites believers.

- Broadcast Media/Internet – Shared gospel instantly. Reaches billions.

- Computers – Organized Church records. Enhances efficiency.

- Air Travel – Bridged global congregations. Gathers saints.

Without the Restoration, the Atonement's power would be lost on us—we need to know it and act on it. If Christ could feel impatient (He probably didn't, but I sure would have been!), His impatience would be during those long years preparing for His appearance to Joseph Smith, eager to restart His work. I'm deeply grateful for Joseph's courage in helping the Lord restore His Church to the earth.

# THE TWELFTH DAY OF CHRISTMAS

*"He shall so come in like manner."*

## The Second Coming of Jesus Christ

"Ye men of Galilee, why stand ye gazing up into heaven? This same Jesus, which is taken up from you into heaven, shall so come in like manner as ye have seen him go into heaven." (Acts 1:11)

So spake the white-robed angels to the eleven apostles as the resurrected Christ ascended from their midst on Olivet. The scriptures abound in predictions of the Lord's return.

By the Second Coming, I am not referring to the personal appearing of the Son of God to the few, such as His visitation to Saul of Tarsus or to Joseph Smith in 1820, and again in the Kirtland Temple in 1836; nor later manifestations to His worthy servants as specifically promised. Nor am I referring to the day He appears to me (see day 13).

I am talking about His future coming in power and great glory, accompanied by hosts of resurrected and glorified beings, to execute judgment upon the earth and to inaugurate a reign of righteousness.

So much has been written about this event, but since it is found in Isaiah and the Book of Revelation, I have no idea how it really is going to take place. It will be pretty cool, however. There is a ton written about the signs of the times and the days leading up to the Second Coming, but I don't want to include all that here. I want to focus on the day when He actually appears.

Bruce McConkie, in the book "Millennial Messiah," helped me gather up the following references and much of the following editorial is his.

The scriptures make it pretty clear that He shall not come in secret. His advent will not be in a manger, near a little village in Judea, among tethered beasts of burden. This time, all the thunders of heaven will herald His approach and that of those who are with Him. "Behold, the Lord cometh with ten thousands of His saints, to execute judgment upon all," as promised by Enoch of old. (Jude 1:14-15.)

This time, He shall come, and every living soul on earth shall know that a new order, of worldwide dimensions, has been ushered in. Thus saith the holy word:

> "The Lord Jesus shall be revealed from heaven with His mighty angels, in flaming fire taking vengeance on them that know not God, and that obey not the gospel of our Lord Jesus Christ." (2 Thes. 1:7-8.)

Does this mean real flaming fire? It is actual, literal fire, fire that burns trees, melts ore, and consumes corruption. It is the same kind of fire that burned in the furnace of Nebuchadnezzar when Shadrach, Meshach, and Abednego were cast into its blazing flames. And though the heat and flames of fire "slew those men" whose lot it was to cast the three Hebrews into its flames, yet, miraculously, upon the bodies of these three, "the fire had no power, nor was a hair of their head singed, neither were their coats changed, nor the smell of fire had passed on them." (Dan. 3:16-27.) Does this mean it can be a selective fire?

And so shall it be at the Second Coming when the same literal fire burns over all the earth. The wicked shall be consumed, and the righteous shall be as though they walked in the furnace of Nebuchadnezzar.

Graphic accounts of the fire and burning that will attend the Second Coming are found in the ancient word. "Our God shall come, and shall not keep silence," acclaims the Psalmist; "a fire shall devour before Him, and it shall be very tempestuous round about Him." (Ps. 50:3.) And also:

> "The Lord reigneth. . . . A fire goeth before Him, and burneth up His enemies round about. His lightnings enlightened the world: the earth saw, and trembled. The hills melted like wax at the presence of the Lord, at the presence of the Lord of the whole earth." (Ps. 97:1-5.)

None of the prophets excel Isaiah in literary craftsmanship and in the use of grand imagery to teach and testify about the God of Israel and His laws.

> "The Lord cometh," Isaiah says, "burning with His anger, and . . . His lips are full of indignation, and His tongue as a devouring fire. . . . And the Lord shall cause His glorious voice to be heard, and shall show the lighting down of His arm, with the indignation of His anger, and with the flame of a devouring fire, with scattering [i.e., with a blast], and tempest, and hailstones." And "the breath of the Lord, like a stream of brimstone," shall kindle the fires that destroy false worship. (Isa. 30:27-33.) "For,

behold, the Lord will come with fire, and with His chariots like
a whirlwind, to render His anger with fury, and His rebuke with
flames of fire. For by fire and by His sword will the Lord plead with
all flesh: and the slain of the Lord shall be many." (Isa. 66:15-16.)

Peter, along with James and John, the other two members of the First
Presidency in their day, saw in vision the transfiguration of the earth. These
three were then with Jesus on Mount Hermon. It was the occasion when
He Himself was also transfigured before them. Speaking of this day of
transfiguration, this millennial day—ushered in, as it will be, by the day of
burning—our revelation says:

"The earth shall be transfigured, even according to the pattern
which was shown unto mine apostles upon the mount; of which
account the fulness ye have not yet received." (D&C 63:20-21.)

Thus, these holy apostles saw the pattern, the way, and the manner in
which the transfiguration of the earth occurred. A part, but not all, of what
they saw, we know.

Knowing how this transfiguration was to take place, having seen it all in
vision, Peter has left us these graphic words: "The heavens and the earth,
which are now," he says, meaning our present earth and the aerial heavens
that surround it, are "reserved unto fire against the day of judgment and
perdition of ungodly men." Then, recording what he and his brethren had
seen on the Mount of Transfiguration, Peter said:

"But the day of the Lord will come as a thief in the night; in
which the heavens shall pass away with a great noise, and the
elements shall melt with fervent heat, the earth also and the
works that are therein shall be burned up."

"Seeing then that all these things shall be dissolved," Peter continues, "what
manner of persons ought ye to be in all holy conversation and godliness,
looking for and hasting unto the coming of the day of God, wherein the
heavens being on fire shall be dissolved, and the elements shall melt with
fervent heat?" Work righteousness or be burned! How persuasive is this
exhortation to walk uprightly before the Lord! "Nevertheless we, according
to His promise, look for new heavens and a new earth, wherein dwelleth
righteousness." The transfiguration shall truly come to pass; the wicked shall
be burned as stubble, and the Lord will reign in millennial splendor among
those that remain.

"Wherefore, beloved, seeing that ye look for such things, be
diligent that ye may be found of Him in peace, without spot, and
blameless." (2 Pet. 3:7-14.)

Isaiah, Amos, Micah, Nahum, and many more all talk about this big, Big, BIG day. It is also then backed up by modern revelation.

> "And also that of element shall melt with fervent heat; and all things shall become new, that my knowledge and glory may dwell upon all the earth." (D&C 101:25.)

I tend to believe that the fire is real, and things will really burn.

I believe the words "the end" refer to the end of the world, not the end of the earth.

The end of the world is not the end of the earth. By the world, we mean the customs, practices, and interests of men as social beings. We mean the social order that prevails among those who live on the earth. We mean the carnality, sensuality, and devilishness that rules in the lives of the wicked and ungodly. We mean the way of life followed by those who love Satan more than God because their deeds are evil.

Worldly people lie and steal and cheat; they take advantage of their neighbor for a word; and they bear false witness, both with the voice of gossip and on the witness stand when they have sworn to speak only the truth. Worldly people rob and plunder and murder. They accept war as a matter of national policy. They are lewd and lascivious. Sex sin is their friend; pornography walks with them; their conversation is profane and vulgar. They include adulterers and homosexuals and those whose thoughts dwell on low and base and sex-oriented things.

The world is evil, carnal, base. It fights the truth, kills the prophets, slays the saints. Worldly people oppose and fight The Church of Jesus Christ of Latter-day Saints because they belong to another kingdom, the kingdom of the devil. The end of the world is the end of all this: it is the end of wickedness; it is the ushering in of a new world, a new age, a new social order—the order of peace and righteousness.

Jesus said:

> "I am not of the world." (John 17:16.)

> "I have overcome the world." (John 16:33.)

To His apostles, He explained:

> "If ye were of the world, the world would love its own: but because ye are not of the world, but I have chosen you out of the world, therefore the world hateth you." (John 15:19.)

And it was the beloved John who counseled:

"Love not the world, neither the things that are in the world. If
any man love the world, the love of the Father is not in him. For
all that is in the world, the lust of the flesh, and the lust of the
eyes, and the pride of life, is not of the Father, but is of the world."

And having so taught, he added these words of wondrous comfort:

"And the world passeth away, and the lust thereof: but he that
doeth the will of God abideth forever." (1 Jn. 2:15-17.)

Jesus Himself said that at His coming, His people would say of Him:

"Blessed is He who cometh in the name of the Lord, in the clouds
of heaven, and all the holy angels with Him."

Since that primeval day when the Lord "laid the foundations of the earth,"
and in which "the morning stars sang together, and all the sons of God
shouted for joy" (Job 38:4-7), since the day of creation's dawn, has there ever
been another time when all the angels of God in heaven have participated in
one single event? Of the day of His return, Jesus also said:

"They shall see the Son of Man coming in the clouds of heaven,
with power and great glory; and whoso treasureth up my word,
shall not be deceived, for the Son of Man shall come, and He shall
send His angels before Him with the great sound of a trumpet,
and they shall gather together the remainder of His elect from
the four winds, from one end of heaven to the other." (JS-M 1:1,
36-37.)

So, this big 12th day—His coming in all His glory—will change everything
except those of us who do His will; we (I hope to be part of this group) will
abide forever. It will be a great day of rejoicing. I don't know much more
about how the rest of this day will roll out. I don't know if we then go home
for dinner or if our houses are melted and we live in a garden. Again, what I
do know is that I need to be vigilant like the five smart virgins and have my
oil and my lamps trimmed. That means I need to study my scriptures, get to
Sunday School, love my neighbors, and a bunch of other things.

But what I really think is that, even despite the greatness of this day when
He gets to come in all His glory, His favorite day is day 13.

# THE THIRTEENTH DAY OF CHRISTMAS

*Bonus Day – consider this a "baker's" 12 days of Christmas.*

### "Son, thou shalt be exalted."

When He takes me in His arms—

When the Lord revealed to Moses the great purpose of life, He expressed Himself in these words:

> "For behold, this is my work and my glory—to bring to pass the immortality and eternal life of man." (Moses 1:39.)

On one side, it is God's work to bring to pass my immortality, yet according to Joseph Smith, I have some responsibility in that work.

> *"You have got to learn how to be Gods yourselves, and to be kings and priests to God." (Teachings of the Prophet Joseph Smith, Deseret Book Co., 1938, p. 346.)*

I want this blessing, and I want it so much I am willing to do my part.

I was born as a spirit son of the Eternal Father, and Jesus Christ is my elder brother in the spirit. Their status is transcendently greater than mine, and I should never even think that I could ever become as they are.

But the scriptures make it very clear that I was born in the lineage of the gods. I have always thought that my Savior would take it as a very personal insult if I ever told Him that even through His atonement, I couldn't rise to the heights of godhood. How could I ever tell Him that His atonement wasn't quite good enough?

Look at what was revealed to Joseph Smith.

> "Then shall they be gods, because they have no end; therefore shall they be from everlasting to everlasting, because they continue; then shall they be above all, because all things are subject unto them. Then shall they be gods, because they have all

power, and the angels are subject unto them." (D&C 132:20.)

The reason I still have hope is that I don't have to know everything. According to the Prophet Joseph, I can take it one step at a time.

> *"When you climb up a ladder, you must begin at the bottom, and ascend step by step, until you arrive at the top; and so it is with the principles of the Gospel—you must begin with the first, and go on until you learn all the principles of exaltation. But it will be a great while after you have passed through the veil before you will have learned them. It is not all to be comprehended in this world; it will be a great work to learn our salvation and exaltation even beyond the grave." (Teachings, p. 348.)*

It is interesting to me that sometimes the Savior refers to us as servants, sometimes friends, and sometimes sons and daughters. I need to spend more time researching to see if there is a pattern. Whichever one is the top of the ladder that Joseph Smith just described is the one I want.

> *"I would exhort you to go on and continue to call upon God until you make your calling and election sure for yourselves, by obtaining this more sure word of prophecy, and wait patiently for the promise until you obtain it." (Teachings, p. 299.)*

There are a few things that stand in my way. We find them in 2 Peter, D&C 4, and in D&C 93. If you don't remember these three scriptures, go look them up. Basically, they are a laundry list of characteristics we need to obtain.

The knowledge of Christ is where we start, and that is basically the emulation of His life and teachings. We begin attaining the virtues found in Jesus' life to which Peter refers. This process starts with sincere repentance, in becoming a member of the true church, then you add to the principles and ordinances that admitted you into the kingdom of God by being diligent in His obedience. Then you add to "faith virtue; and to virtue knowledge;

> "And to knowledge temperance; and to temperance patience; and to patience godliness;

> "And to godliness brotherly kindness; and to brotherly kindness charity." (2 Pet. 1:5–7; see also Teachings, p. 305.)

> "Till we all come in the unity of the faith, and of the knowledge of the Son of God, unto a perfect man, unto the measure of the stature of the fulness of Christ:" (Eph. 4:13.)

To be in the position of "Well Done," I will, according to the scriptures and the teachings of Joseph Smith, have power to overcome all enemies in this world (meaning the vices which are the opposites of gospel virtues) and "the knowledge to triumph over all evil spirits in the world to come." (Teachings, p. 297.) And that the triumph over one's enemies would come only through a knowledge of the priesthood. (See Teachings, p. 305.)

The knowledge of the priesthood refers to obedience to "the mysteries of the kingdom"—the higher ordinances of the gospel, which I consider to be the ordinances of the temple. In a Sunday School class, it was mentioned that the mysteries and ordinances are the same thing when you consider the Greek, Hebrew, and other translations of the words. This would make sense as you look at these scriptures.

> "And the disciples came, and said unto him, Why speakest thou unto them in parables?
>
> He answered and said unto them, Because it is given unto you to know the mysteries of the kingdom of heaven, but to them it is not given.
>
> For whosoever hath, to him shall be given, and he shall have more abundance: but whosoever hath not, from him shall be taken away even that he hath. Therefore speak I to them in parables: because they seeing see not; and hearing they hear not, neither do they understand." (Matt. 13:10–13.)
>
> "And now Alma began to expound these things unto him, saying: It is given unto many to know the mysteries of God; nevertheless they are laid under a strict command that they shall not impart only according to the portion of his word which he doth grant unto the children of men, according to the heed and diligence which they give unto him." (Alma 12:9.)
>
> "And I have given unto him the keys of the mystery of those things which have been sealed, even things which were from the foundation of the world, and the things which shall come from this time until the time of my coming, if he abide in me, and if not, another will I plant in his stead." (D&C 35:18.)
>
> "But unto him that keepeth my commandments I will give the mysteries of my kingdom, and the same shall be in him a well of living water, springing up unto everlasting life." (D&C 63:23.)
>
> "Behold, thou shalt observe all these things, and great shall be thy reward; for unto you it is given to know the mysteries of the kingdom, but unto the world it is not given to know them." (D&C 42:65.)

Joseph Smith said:

> *"The question is frequently asked, 'Can we not be saved without going through with all those ordinances?' I would answer, No, not the fulness of salvation. ...*
>
> *"If a man gets a fullness of the priesthood of God, he has to get it in the same way that Jesus Christ obtained it, and that was by keeping all the commandments and obeying all the ordinances of the house of the Lord." (Teachings, pp. 331, 308.)*

This is going to be hard work. Joseph Smith continues.

> *"From the first existence of man, the faith necessary unto the enjoyment of life and salvation never could be obtained without the sacrifice of all earthly things. It was through this sacrifice, and this only, that God has ordained that men should enjoy eternal life; and it is through the medium of the sacrifice of all earthly things that men do actually know that they are doing the things that are well pleasing in the sight of God. When a man has offered in sacrifice all that he has for the truth's sake, not even withholding his life, and believing before God that he has been called to make this sacrifice because he seeks to do his will, he does know, most assuredly, that God does and will accept his sacrifice and offering, and that he has not, nor will not seek his face in vain. Under these circumstances, then, he can obtain the faith necessary for him to lay hold on eternal life." (Lectures on Faith, 6:58; see also D&C 98:11–15 and Teachings, p. 322.)*
>
> *"After a person has faith in Christ, repents of his sins, and is baptized for the remission of his sins and receives the Holy Ghost (by the laying on of hands), which is the first Comforter, then let him continue to humble himself before God, hungering and thirsting after righteousness, and living by every word of God, and the Lord will soon say unto him, Son, thou shalt be exalted. When the Lord has thoroughly proved him, and finds that the man is determined to serve Him at all hazards, then the man will find his calling and his election made sure." (Teachings, p. 150.)*
>
> *Such a person eventually receives godhood and becomes a member of the "church of the Firstborn." (D&C 76:54.)*

If you eyes started to glaze over, the past twelve paragraphs, let me sum up:

## Knowledge of the Priesthood and Mysteries:

The knowledge of the priesthood involves obedience to the "mysteries of the kingdom," equated with the higher gospel ordinances, particularly temple ordinances, as supported by translations of Greek, Hebrew, and other terms linking mysteries and ordinances (Matt. 13:10–13; Alma 12:9; D&C 35:18, 42:65, 63:23).

**Necessity of Ordinances for Salvation:** Joseph Smith taught that the fulness of salvation requires adherence to all gospel ordinances, obtained through keeping commandments and participating in temple ordinances, as exemplified by Jesus Christ (Teachings, pp. 331, 308).

**Sacrifice for Eternal Life:** Achieving eternal life demands the sacrifice of all earthly things, which, when offered with faith and obedience to God's will, confirms one's actions are pleasing to God and grants the faith needed to attain eternal life (Lectures on Faith, 6:58; D&C 98:11–15; Teachings, p. 322).

**Path to Exaltation and the Church of the Firstborn:** Through faith, repentance, baptism, receiving the Holy Ghost, and ongoing humility and righteousness, a person can have their calling and election made sure, ultimately achieving godhood and membership in the "church of the Firstborn" (Teachings, p. 150; D&C 76:54).

As I mentioned, I don't have to know everything, but there are some things that I must know. In 1844, Joseph Smith taught that *"it is the first principle of the Gospel to know for a certainty the Character of God, and to know that we may converse with him as one man converses with another."* (Teachings, p. 345.)

Ten years earlier, the Lectures on Faith, which Joseph Smith directed and approved, taught that to acquire faith unto salvation, one needs a correct idea of God's character, perfections, and attributes, and that one needs to know that the course of life one is pursuing is according to God's will. (Lectures on Faith, 3:2–5.) He also added, *"If men do not comprehend the character of God, they do not comprehend themselves." (Teachings, p. 343.)*

The Prophet Joseph Smith indicated that when a person has been proved of the Lord by *"hungering and thirsting after righteousness, and living by every word of God,"* he may then have the privilege of receiving the Second Comforter. This Comforter is the presence of the Lord Jesus Christ, *"and the visions of the heavens will be opened unto him, and the Lord will teach him face to face."* Joseph Smith went on to say that this was the condition of a number of the ancient saints, naming Isaiah, Ezekiel, John the Revelator, Paul, and *"all the saints who held communion with the general assembly and Church of the Firstborn." (See Teachings, pp. 150–51.)*

These promised blessings are personal, yes available globally but promised individually. Here is a smattering of promised examples.

- "And I soon go to the place of my rest, which is with my Redeemer; for I know that in him I shall rest. And I rejoice in the day when my mortal shall put on immortality, and shall stand before him; then shall I see his face with pleasure, and he will say unto me: Come unto me, ye blessed, there is a place prepared for you in the mansions of my Father. Amen." (Enos 1:27.)

• "Thou art my servant; and I covenant with thee that thou shalt have eternal life; and thou shalt serve me and go forth in my name, and shalt gather together my sheep." (Mosiah 26:20.)

• "And again we bear record—for we saw and heard, and this is the testimony of the gospel of Christ concerning them who shall come forth in the resurrection of the just—

• They are they who received the testimony of Jesus, and believed on his name and were baptized after the manner of his burial, being buried in the water in his name, and this according to the commandment which he has given—

• That by keeping the commandments they might be washed and cleansed from all their sins, and receive the Holy Spirit by the laying on of the hands of him who is ordained and sealed unto this power;

• And who overcome by faith, and are sealed by the Holy Spirit of promise, which the Father sheds forth upon all those who are just and true.

• They are they who are the church of the Firstborn. They are they into whose hands the Father has given all things—

• They are they who are priests and kings, who have received of his fulness, and of his glory;

• And are priests of the Most High, after the order of Melchizedek, which was after the order of Enoch, which was after the order of the Only Begotten Son. Wherefore, as it is written, they are gods, even the sons of God—

• Wherefore, all things are theirs, whether life or death, or things present, or things to come, all are theirs and they are Christ's, and Christ is God's.

• And they shall overcome all things." (D&C 76:50–60.)

• We are told that many Saints have made their calling and election sure.

• "That when he shall finish his work I may receive him unto myself, even as I did my servant David Patten, who is with me at this time, and also my servant Edward Partridge, and also my aged servant Joseph Smith, Sen., who sitteth with Abraham at his right hand, and blessed and holy is he, for he is mine." (D&C 124:19.)

This is what the Prophet said about William Clayton:

- "Your life is hid with Christ in God, and so are many others. Nothing but the unpardonable sin can prevent you from inheriting eternal life for you are sealed up by the power of the Priesthood unto eternal life, having taken the step necessary for that purpose." (History of the Church, 5:391.)

President Marion G. Romney, as a member of the Council of the Twelve, admonished the Saints in general conference to make their calling and election sure and said:

- "The fullness of eternal life is not attainable in mortality, but the peace which is its harbinger and which comes as a result of making one's calling and election sure is attainable in this life. The Lord has promised that '... he who doeth the works of righteousness shall receive his reward, even peace in this world, and eternal life in the world to come.' (D&C 59:23.)

To sum up, my goal is to obey the Prophet Joseph Smith:

> *"Then I would exhort you to go on and continue to call upon God until you make your calling and election sure for yourselves, by obtaining this more sure word of prophecy, and wait patiently for the promise until you obtain it." (Teachings, p. 299.)*

I wish to thank Roy W. Doxey for an article in the July 1976 Ensign entitled "Accepted of the Lord: The Doctrine of Making Your Calling and Election Sure," which showed me where to get all these great quotes from Joseph Smith.

It's tough to consider myself anyone of consequence when I look at the universe and consider all the children God has made. If it weren't for the fact that my prayers always get answered and I see His hand in my life every day, I would wonder if it was all real. I testify that it is real, that Jesus is the Christ and is my Savior. I don't know why or how, but I know He loves me and is looking forward to my day with Him.

Here is one more teaching of the Prophet Joseph that backs up my hope to become like my Savior.

The Prophet explained that *"God himself was once as we are now, and is an exalted man, and sits enthroned in yonder heavens"; that "he was once a man like us; yea, that God himself, the Father of us all, dwelt on an earth, the same as Jesus Christ himself did"; and that he "worked out his kingdom with fear and trembling." (Teachings, p. 343.)*

Through the Prophet, we learn that we "are begotten sons and daughters unto God" and that Christ is the Firstborn. (D&C 76:24; see D&C 93:21–22; Heb. 12:7–9.) As God's children, we may become gods ourselves through

Christ's atonement and the plan of salvation, being joint heirs of Christ of "all that [the] Father hath." (D&C 84:38; see also Rom. 8:17; D&C 76:58–60; D&C 132:19–21.)

Along with these concepts is the concept of divine parents, including an exalted Mother who stands beside God the Father. (The concepts of husband and wife becoming gods, sharing in their kingdom, and continuing to bear children are delineated in Doctrine and Covenants 131:1–4; 132:19–20.

These things suggest the concept of an exalted Mother. Eliza R. Snow's poem "O My Father," written in 1843, establishes that the doctrine was known early in Church history. For further information, see the 1909 First Presidency message "The Origin of Man," in Messages of the First Presidency, comp. James R. Clark, 6 vols., 1965–75, 4:203–5.)

Let me conclude with this verse:

> "For I am the Lord thy God, and will be with thee even unto the end of the world, and through all eternity; for verily I seal upon you your exaltation, and prepare a throne for you in the kingdom of my Father, with Abraham your father." (D&C 132:49.)

He is talking to you and me! Let's not blow it.

# APPENDIX

**Chapter Three**

There is a lot to learn just by reading chapter 3 of Genesis. I have included it here.

1. NOW the serpent was more subtle than any beast of the field which the LORD God had made. And he said unto the woman, Yea, hath God said, Ye shall not eat of every tree of the garden?

2. And the woman said unto the serpent, We may eat of the fruit of the trees of the garden:

3. But of the fruit of the tree which is in the midst of the garden, God hath said, Ye shall not eat of it, neither shall ye touch it, lest ye die.

4. And the serpent said unto the woman, Ye shall not surely die:

5. For God doth know that in the day ye eat thereof, then your eyes shall be opened, and ye shall be as gods, knowing good and evil.

6. And when the woman saw that the tree was good for food, and that it was pleasant to the eyes, and a tree to be desired to make one wise, she took of the fruit thereof, and did eat, and gave also unto her husband with her; and he did eat.

7. And the eyes of them both were opened, and they knew that they were naked; and they sewed fig leaves together, and made themselves aprons.

8. And they heard the voice of the LORD God walking in the garden in the cool of the day: and Adam and his wife hid themselves from the presence of the LORD God amongst the trees of the garden.

9. And the LORD God called unto Adam, and said unto him, Where art thou?

10. And he said, I heard thy voice in the garden, and I was afraid, because I was naked; and I hid myself.

11. And he said, Who told thee that thou wast naked? Hast thou eaten of the tree, whereof I commanded thee that thou shouldest not eat?

12. And the man said, The woman whom thou gavest to be with me, she gave me of the tree, and I did eat.

13. And the LORD God said unto the woman, What is this that thou hast done? And the woman said, The serpent beguiled me, and I did eat.

14. And the LORD God said unto the serpent, Because thou hast done this, thou art cursed above all cattle, and above every beast of the field; upon thy belly shalt thou go, and dust shalt thou eat all the days of thy life:

15. And I will put enmity between thee and the woman, and between thy seed and her seed; it shall bruise thy head, and thou shalt bruise his heel.

16. Unto the woman he said, I will greatly multiply thy sorrow and thy conception; in sorrow thou shalt bring forth children; and thy desire shall be to thy husband, and he shall rule over thee.

17. And unto Adam he said, Because thou hast hearkened unto the voice of thy wife, and hast eaten of the tree, of which I commanded thee, saying, Thou shalt not eat of it: cursed is the ground for thy sake; in sorrow shalt thou eat of it all the days of thy life;

18. Thorns also and thistles shall it bring forth to thee; and thou shalt eat the herb of the field;

19. In the sweat of thy face shalt thou eat bread, till thou return unto the ground; for out of it wast thou taken: for dust thou art, and unto dust shalt thou return.

20. And Adam called his wife's name Eve; because she was the mother of all living.

21. Unto Adam also and to his wife did the LORD God make coats of skins, and clothed them.

22. And the LORD God said, Behold, the man is become as one of us, to know good and evil: and now, lest he put forth his hand, and take also of the tree of life, and eat, and live for ever:

23. Therefore the LORD God sent him forth from the Garden of Eden, to till the ground from whence he was taken.

24. So he drove out the man; and he placed at the east of the garden of Eden Cherubims, and a flaming sword which turned every way, to keep the way of the tree of life.

Throughout the scriptures, the fall of Adam is taught and referred to. Here are just a few of the references from all the standard works.

• In the day that thou eatest thereof thou shalt surely die, (Gen. 2: 17 , Moses 3: 17).

• She took of the fruit thereof, and did eat, Gen. 3: 6 (Moses 4: 12).

• As in Adam all die, even so in Christ shall all be made alive, 1 Cor. 15: 22.

• All mankind were in a lost and in a fallen state, 1 Ne. 10: 6.

• The way is prepared from the fall of man, 2 Ne. 2: 4.

• After Adam and Eve had partaken of the forbidden fruit, they were driven out of the Garden of Eden, 2 Ne. 2: 19.

• Adam fell that men might be, 2 Ne. 2: 15-26.

• The natural man is an enemy to God, and has been from the fall of Adam, Mosiah 3: 19.

• Aaron taught Lamoni's father about the Fall, Alma 22: 12-14.

• There must be an atonement made or else all mankind are fallen and lost, Alma 34: 9.

• Our first parents were cut off both temporally and spiritually from the presence of the Lord, Alma 42: 2-15 (Hel. 14: 16).

• Because of the Fall our natures have become evil, (Ether 3: 2.)

• By the transgression of these holy laws man became fallen man, D&C 20: 20 (D&C 29: 34-44).

• As thou hast fallen thou mayest be redeemed, Moses 5: 9-12.

• By reason of transgression cometh the Fall, Moses 6: 59.

• Men will be punished for their own sins, A of F 1: 2. Among other things that modern revelation and our non- biblical records makes clear that the fall is a blessing, and that Adam and Eve should be honored in their station as the first parents of the earth. Significant references are: 2 Ne. 2: 15-16; 2 Ne. 9: 6-21; Mosiah 3: 11-16; Alma 22: 12-14; Alma 42: 2-15; D&C 29: 34-44; Moses 5: 9-13.

## Chapter Five

I have included here a presentation by Kent Jackson along with all the references, sources, footnotes etc.. Read it if you wish. Its long but pretty fascinating. If you don't feel like it, just move on to day 6. Day 6 was also a pretty good day for our Savior.

**"Never Have I Showed Myself unto Man"**: A Suggestion for Understanding Ether 3:15 by Kent P. Jackson

Ether 3:15 contains a statement from the Lord that sets the brother of Jared apart from everyone who had lived on earth up to his time: "Never have I showed myself unto man whom I have created, for never has man believed in me as thou hast." The uniqueness of Mahonri Moriancumer's faith justified the uniqueness of the Lord's revelation to him. Never, the Lord told him, had anyone experienced such a manifestation--a statement made even more remarkable when we consider that such great individuals as Adam, Eve, Enoch, and Noah had preceded the brother of Jared, and each of these, according to the scriptures, had conversed with God.

In this brief essay I will present some ideas concerning the Lord's statement in Ether 3:15. After sketching the common explanations proposed for the verse, I will suggest an alternative point of view that is, in my opinion, true to the text and consistent with what we know of the doctrine of God.

In response to the brother of Jared's efforts to provide light for the Jaredite barges, the Lord first revealed to him His finger (Ether 3:6) and then finally His entire person (Ether 3:13-16). In the process He taught him much concerning the nature of Deity and revealed His own identity as well: "Because of thy faith thou hast seen that I shall take upon me flesh and blood" (Ether 3:9) "Behold this body, which ye now behold, is the body of my spirit; . . . and even as I appear unto thee to be in the spirit will I appear unto my people in the flesh" (Ether 3:16). Moroni, the narrator of the account, provided a valuable summary and makes clear the identity of the deity who spoke: "Jesus showed himself unto this man in the spirit, even after the manner and in the likeness of the same body even as he showed himself unto the Nephites" (Ether 3:17).

Mahonri was speaking with the premortal Jesus Christ, who would be born on earth over two thousand years later, receive a physical body, and while in the flesh, atone for the sins of the world. We cannot tell from the account what Mahonri knew about the nature of God or the mission of Christ prior to his vision, but it appears in verse 8 that he was startled to see what he thought was a body of "flesh and blood." The Lord's comments in verse 16 seem to make it clear that it was a body of spirit that the prophet saw.

The unprecedented faith of the brother of Jared is mentioned both by Jesus and by Moroni as the factor that led to the unprecedented revelation. The Lord said, "Never has man come before me with such exceeding faith as thou hast" (Ether 3:9). Moroni added further emphasis: "Having this perfect knowledge of God, he could not be kept from within the veil. . . . The Lord could not withhold anything from him, for he knew that the Lord could show him all things" (Ether 3:20, 26). The key statement from the Lord is found in Ether 3:15a: "Never have I showed myself unto man whom I have created, for

123

never has man believed in me as thou hast."

Whatever the first clause of verse 15 means, it is clear that there was something extraordinary about this appearance of the Lord to the brother of Jared. Yet we know from the scriptures that others had in fact seen God. Adam and Eve conversed with the Lord in "the presence of the Lord God" while in the Garden of Eden (Moses 4:14-27) Adam and many others saw him in a great meeting not long before Adam's death (D&C 107:53-54) Enoch "saw the Lord" and spoke with him "even as a man talketh one with another, face to face" (Moses 7:4) and Noah and his sons "walked with God" (Moses 8:27). Our problem, then, is to determine the meaning of the Lord's statement to the brother of Jared in light of what we know of these other pre-Jaredite theophanies.

The most common approach to understanding Ether 3:15 a proposes that the Lord's statement has reference to the degree to which he revealed himself to the brother of Jared. President Joseph Fielding Smith stated this position as follows:

I have always considered Ether 3:15 to mean that the Savior stood before the Brother of Jared plainly, distinctly, and showed him his whole body and explained to him that he was a spirit. In his appearance to Adam and Enoch, he had not made himself manifest in such a familiar way. His appearances to earlier prophets had not been with that same fulness.

The scriptural accounts of talking face to face and of walking with God should not be interpreted in the sense that the Savior stood before those prophets and revealed his whole person. That he may have done so at later periods in the cases of Abraham and Moses is possible, but he had not done so in that fulness in the antediluvian days. For the Brother of Jared he removed the veil completely. He had never showed himself to man before in the manner and way he did to that prophet.

Elder Bruce R. McConkie interpreted the verse by restating it as follows: "'Never have I showed myself in the manner and form now involved; never has there been such a complete revelation of the nature and kind of being I am; never before has the veil been lifted completely so that a mortal man has been able to see my spirit body in the full and complete sense of the word.' This approach is expressed in similar terms by other Latter-day Saint commentators.

As another possible interpretation, Sidney B. Sperry suggested that the word "man" in Ether 3:15 may mean "unbelieving man." Never had the Lord shown himself to those who did not believe on his name, whereas to the faithful--presumably including individuals like Adam and Enoch--he had indeed shown himself as he did to Mahonri Moriancumer.

Daniel H. Ludlow pointed out one aspect of the brother of Jared's experience that perhaps was unprecedented and may have something to do with the statement in Ether 3:15. Emphasizing verses 19, 20 ("he could not be kept from within the veil"), and 26 ("the Lord could not withhold anything from him"), Ludlow wrote that the Lord "never had to show himself unto man before."

This explanation probably tells us more about why the Lord gave him this unique experience than what was unique about it.

These proposals are not, of course, mutually exclusive, and a correct understanding of the verse may entail elements of more than one of them. A starting point for interpretation is the idea that the Lord showed himself to the brother of Jared to a greater degree than to any earlier prophet. Yet that interpretation requires the addition of several modifiers to the Lord's seemingly unequivocal and absolute statement, "Never have I showed myself unto man whom I have created." I would like to propose an explanation that builds on this interpretation yet allows us to take the Lord's statement literally as it stands.

In order to avoid ambiguity in the following discussion, I will follow traditional Latter-day Saint usage and employ the name "Elohim" exclusively for God, the Father of our spirits, and "Jehovah" exclusively for the Lord Jesus Christ. This approach is necessary for clarity because the scriptures refer to Christ as both "God" and "the Father."

In Ether 3 the brother of Jared was speaking with Jehovah, who, according to King Benjamin, is "the Lord Omnipotent who reigneth, who was, and is from all eternity to all eternity. . . . the Father of heaven and earth, the Creator of all things from the beginning" (Mosiah 3:5, 8; see also Alma 11:39). Under the direction of Elohim, Jehovah is God of the universe, presiding over all things. Having been endowed by Elohim with infinite power, glory, and authority, Jehovah is the Father, as the Book of Mormon designates him frequently. He is God who speaks to the prophets, who establishes and reveals laws for the blessing of the world, and who directs the affairs of the human family.

We know also that Jehovah is the same being who later was born into the world as Jesus Christ. He became a being of dual nature: he is both Father and Son as he is also both God and Man (see D&C 93:3-4). Prior to his birth, he was the Lord Jehovah (Father, God); while he walked the earth, he was also the mortal Jesus Christ (Son, Man).

The standard Latter-day Saint view of Jehovah's role as God was expressed by President Joseph Fielding Smith:

Each of the above-mentioned explanations of Ether 3:15a presupposes a theology similar to that of Joseph Fielding Smith: "All revelation since the fall has come through Jesus Christ. . . . The Father [Elohim] has never dealt with man directly and personally since the fall, and he has never appeared except to introduce and bear record of the Son." Assuming that such is the case, this appearance to the brother of Jared is the first recorded manifestation of Jehovah in which he appeared and identified himself as the Son. Elsewhere the scriptures record him appearing or speaking as God the Father (for example, Moses 6:50-52, 58-59; 7:4, 32-33, 39; see also 1:1-6). But to the brother of Jared he said, "Behold, I am Jesus Christ. I am the Father and the Son. In me shall all mankind have life, and that eternally, even they who shall believe on my name; and they shall become my sons and my daughters. And never have I showed myself unto man whom I have created, for never has man believed in me as thou hast" (Ether 3:14-15).

The uniqueness of this situation lies in the fact that Jehovah appeared to Mahonri Moriancumer in his role as Jesus Christ--rather than as the Father. Never before, as far as we can tell from the scriptures, had Jesus Christ shown himself unto man. (And, interestingly, nowhere else in the scriptures do we have a clear example of Jehovah appearing as Jesus until his coming in the flesh.) As Moroni reported, "Having this perfect knowledge of God, he could not be kept from within the veil; therefore he saw Jesus" (Ether 3:20). To the brother of Jared, Christ revealed his complete nature: God who would become Man--Jehovah, the Father, who would become Jesus, the Son.

Perhaps the unprecedented nature of this appearance is a reason why the Lord commanded that the account not be made known in the world until after his mortal ministry (Ether 3:21).

BYU Studies, vol. 30 (1990), Number 3 - Summer 1990" Kent P. Jackson is an associate professor of ancient scripture at Brigham Young University. All italics in scripture citations in this article are my own emphasis.


# Chapter Seven
## Authority in the Ministry
### Prior to the Mosaic Dispensation

- Adam was commissioned to teach and was after the order of God (Moses 6:57–58, 67).

- The Lord commanded Noah to build the ark (Genesis 6:13–14, 22; 7:1).

- Noah was ordained after the Lord's own order (Moses 8:19).

- The Lord commanded Abraham and entered into covenant with him (Genesis 12:1; 15:9; 17:1–9).

- Abraham became a high priest (Abraham 1:2–3).

- The Lord covenanted with Abraham concerning the priesthood (Abraham 2:9–11).

- Melchizedek was priest of the Most High God (Genesis 14:18–20; Alma 13:18).

- The priesthood was established as eternal after the order of Melchizedek (Psalm 110:4; Hebrews 5:6–10; 6:20; 7:1–3).

- The Lord covenanted with Isaac (Genesis 26:2–5).

- The Lord covenanted with Jacob (Genesis 28:10–15).

## Authority to Moses and Others

- Moses was commissioned to deliver Israel (Exodus 3:4–17).

Moses was given divine authority before Pharaoh (Exodus 7:1).

- Jethro, priest of Midian, conferred the Holy Priesthood upon Moses (Exodus 18; Doctrine and Covenants 84:6).

- Joshua was ordained under the hand of Moses (Numbers 27:18–23; Deuteronomy 34:9).

## Unauthorized Ministry and Retribution

- Punishment came upon those who presumed to officiate without authority (Numbers 16; 1 Chronicles 13:10; 1 Samuel 13:5–14; 2 Chronicles 26).

## Priestly Organization in Israel

- Priests were anointed and consecrated to minister (Numbers 3:3).

- Levites were appointed to assist (Numbers 3:9).

- Seventy elders were called and endowed with the Spirit (Numbers 11:16, 25).

- The Lord chose specific men to minister (Deuteronomy 21:5).

- Israel was promised the title "Priests of the Lord" (Isaiah 61:6).

## Ordained Prophets

- Jeremiah was ordained and given the Lord's words (Jeremiah 1:4–9).

- The word of the Lord came expressly to Ezekiel the priest (Ezekiel 1:3).

- Haggai spoke as the Lord's messenger (Haggai 1:13).

- The word of the Lord came to Zechariah (Zechariah 1:1).

- The priest is the messenger of the Lord of Hosts (Malachi 2:7).

## John the Baptist

- John the Baptist was ordained by an angel at eight days old, prior to his ministry (Doctrine and Covenants 84:28).

- Authority Conferred by Jesus Christ During His Mortal Ministry

- Jesus gave power to the Twelve (Matthew 10:1).

- He ordained Twelve Apostles (Mark 3:14; Luke 6:13).

- Jesus declared that He chose and ordained His disciples (John 15:16; 17:18).

- He appointed and sent out Seventy (Luke 10:1, 17).

- Peter was given the keys of the kingdom (Matthew 16:19).

- The Apostles were commissioned to baptize and teach (Matthew 28:19–20).

Authority was given to remit or retain sins (John 20:21–23).

## Ordination in the Days of the Apostles

- Matthias was chosen and numbered with the Twelve (Acts 1:21–26).

- Seven men were ordained by the laying on of hands (Acts 6:2–6).

- Philip ministered with authority, followed by signs (Acts 8:5–12; Acts 6:5).

- Peter and John administered higher ordinances to the Samaritans (Acts 8:14–17).

- Barnabas and Saul were set apart by the laying on of hands (Acts 13:1–3).

- Elders were ordained in every church (Acts 14:23; Titus 1:5).

- Paul was called and ordained an apostle (Romans 1:1, 5; 1 Corinthians 1:1).

- Preaching requires divine sending (Romans 10:14–15).

- Paul testified of his ordination as preacher and apostle (1 Timothy 2:7; 2 Timothy 1:11).

- Spiritual gifts were conferred by prophecy and laying on of hands (1

• Timothy 4:14; 2 Timothy 1:6).

• Saints were called a royal priesthood (1 Peter 2:9).

• Christ gave apostles, prophets, and other offices to the Church (Ephesians 4:11).

• Jesus Christ is the great High Priest after the order of Melchizedek (Hebrews 5:1–8).

• Those who speak should speak as the oracles of God (1 Peter 4:11).

## Book of Mormon Authority

• Nephi was called to be a ruler and teacher (1 Nephi 2:22; 3:29; 2 Nephi 5:19).

• Nephi consecrated Jacob and Joseph as priests (2 Nephi 5:26).

• Jacob was ordained after the holy order of God (2 Nephi 6:2).

• Alma was consecrated high priest over the Church (Alma 4:4; 8:23; 16:5).

• The high priesthood was after the order of the Son of God (Alma 13:1–19).

• Alma ordained priests and elders by the laying on of hands (Alma 6:1).

• Authority was exercised by those ordained after the holy order of God (Alma 49:30).

• Ancient servants were called after the holy order (Ether 12:10).

• Christ gave the Twelve power to bestow the Holy Ghost (3 Nephi 18:36–37; Moroni 2).

• Other disciples were ordained (4 Nephi 1:14).

• Disciples ordained priests and teachers (Moroni 3).

## Restoration of Priesthood Authority

• Aaronic Priesthood conferred upon Joseph Smith and Oliver Cowdery by John the Baptist (Doctrine and Covenants 13).

• The Lord declared His authority and that of His servants (Doctrine and Covenants 1:6).

• Elijah was promised to reveal priesthood authority (Doctrine and Covenants 2:1).

• Joseph Smith and Oliver Cowdery ordained one another by

commandment (Joseph Smith—History 1:71).

• Ordination must be performed by one holding authority (Doctrine and Covenants 42:11).

• Bishops must be high priests, except literal descendants of Aaron (Doctrine and Covenants 68:14–21).

• Through the priesthood comes salvation to Israel (Doctrine and Covenants 86:11).

• Revelation outlining priesthood lineage and duties was given (Doctrine and Covenants 84).

• Those ordained and sent preach by divine authority (Doctrine and Covenants 50:17; 68:8).

• The higher priesthood was taken from Israel in Moses's day (Doctrine and Covenants 84:25–26).

• Faithfulness in both priesthoods makes one a son of Moses and Aaron (Doctrine and Covenants 84:33–34).

• Warning given to those who reject the priesthood (Doctrine and Covenants 84:42).

• The Twelve were called to preach the gospel worldwide (Doctrine and Covenants 18:27–29).

• The Twelve preside as a traveling high council; the Seventy act under their direction (Doctrine and Covenants 107:23, 33–34).

• Revelation on priesthood quorums and duties was given (Doctrine and Covenants 107).

• Only one man at a time holds the sealing keys (Doctrine and Covenants 132:7).

• The same priesthood existing in the beginning will exist in the end (Moses 6:7).

• Abraham received the priesthood of his fathers (Abraham 1:18, 31).

## Chapter Eight

Below is a detailed day-by-day outline of Jesus Christ's last week, starting with the Saturday night dinner where Mary anoints His feet and ending with His resurrection, based on the King James Version of the New Testament. This timeline follows the traditional Passion Week framework, adjusted to begin with the anointing on Saturday (six days before Passover, per John 12:1). I'll include key events, teachings, parables, and scriptural references for each day. Note that some events' exact days are debated, but this aligns with a widely accepted chronology, with the crucifixion on Friday (though the Thursday crucifixion case was addressed earlier).

## Day 1 – Saturday: The Anointing at Bethany

- Jesus arrives in Bethany six days before Passover and attends a supper at the house of Simon the leper (John 12:1; Matthew 26:6; Mark 14:3).

- Mary, sister of Martha and Lazarus, anoints Jesus with costly spikenard and wipes His feet with her hair (John 12:3).

- Judas Iscariot objects to the "waste," but Jesus defends Mary, declaring the anointing a preparation for His burial and a perpetual memorial (John 12:4–8; Matthew 26:7–13; Mark 14:4–9).

**Teaching:** Devotion to Christ outweighs material concerns; Jesus openly acknowledges His approaching death.

## Day 2 – Sunday: Triumphal Entry (Palm Sunday)

- Jesus enters Jerusalem riding a donkey, fulfilling prophecy (Matthew 21:1–7; Zechariah 9:9).

- Crowds greet Him with palm branches, shouting "Hosanna" and proclaiming Him King (Matthew 21:8–11; Mark 11:8–10; John 12:12–15).

- Jesus weeps over Jerusalem, foretelling its destruction (Luke 19:41–44).

**Teaching:** Christ enters as a humble King; His compassion contrasts with the city's coming judgment.

## Day 3 – Monday: The Fig Tree and the Cleansing of the Temple

- Jesus curses a barren fig tree, symbolizing fruitless faith (Matthew 21:18–19; Mark 11:12–14).

- He enters the temple and drives out money changers, declaring it a house of prayer corrupted by greed (Matthew 21:12–13; Mark 11:15–17; Luke 19:45–46).

**Teaching:** God condemns religious hypocrisy and defends pure worship.

## Day 4 – Tuesday: Teaching, Parables, and the Olivet Discourse

- The fig tree is found withered; Jesus teaches about faith and prayer (Matthew 21:20–22; Mark 11:20–26).

- Religious leaders challenge Jesus's authority; He exposes their insincerity (Matthew 21:23–27; Mark 11:27–33; Luke 20:1–8).

- Jesus teaches multiple parables:
    - The Two Sons (Matthew 21:28–32)
    - The Wicked Husbandmen (Matthew 21:33–46; Mark 12:1–12; Luke 20:9–19)
    - The Marriage Feast (Matthew 22:1–14)

- Jesus answers questions on tribute to Caesar (Matthew 22:15–22; Mark 12:13–17; Luke 20:20–26).

- He affirms the resurrection when questioned by the Sadducees (Matthew 22:23–33; Mark 12:18–27; Luke 20:27–40).

- Jesus teaches the Greatest Commandment (Matthew 22:34–40; Mark 12:28–34).

- He pronounces woes upon the scribes and Pharisees for hypocrisy (Matthew 23:1–39; Mark 12:38–40; Luke 20:45–47).

- Jesus praises the widow's mite as true sacrifice (Mark 12:41–44; Luke 21:1–4).

- On the Mount of Olives, Jesus delivers the Olivet Discourse, prophesying Jerusalem's destruction and His return (Matthew 24–25; Mark 13; Luke 21).

- Parable of the Ten Virgins (Matthew 25:1–13)

- Parable of the Talents (Matthew 25:14–30)

- The Sheep and the Goats (Matthew 25:31–46)

**Teaching:** Faithfulness, readiness, humility, and accountability before God.

## Day 5 – Wednesday: Rest and the Betrayal Plot

- Jesus remains largely silent and withdrawn, likely resting in Bethany (no direct public record).

- Judas conspires with the chief priests to betray Jesus for thirty pieces of silver (Matthew 26:1–5, 14–16; Mark 14:1–2, 10–11; Luke 22:1–6).

**Teaching:** None recorded; betrayal quietly unfolds.

## Day 6 – Thursday: The Last Supper and Gethsemane

- Jesus sends disciples to prepare the Passover (Matthew 26:17–19; Mark 14:12–16; Luke 22:7–13).

- During the Last Supper:

- Jesus washes the disciples' feet, teaching service (John 13:4–17).

- He institutes the sacrament of bread and wine (Matthew 26:26–28; Mark 14:22–24; Luke 22:19–20).

- He predicts Judas's betrayal and Peter's denial (Matthew 26:21–35; John 13:21–38).

- He delivers His farewell discourse and prays for His disciples (John 14–17).

- In Gethsemane, Jesus prays in agony and submits to the Father's will (Matthew 26:36–39; Mark 14:32–36; Luke 22:39–44).

- Judas betrays Jesus; He is arrested (Matthew 26:47–56; Mark 14:43–52; Luke 22:47–53; John 18:1–11).

**Teaching:** Love, humility, obedience, and submission to God's will.

## Day 7 – Friday: Trials, Crucifixion, and Burial (Good Friday)

- Jesus is tried before Annas, Caiaphas, Pilate, and Herod (Matthew 26:57–27:31; Mark 14:53–15:20; Luke 22:54–23:25; John 18–19:16).

- He is crucified at Golgotha and dies about the ninth hour (Matthew 27:32–56; Mark 15:21–41; Luke 23:26–49; John 19:17–37).

- Jesus is buried in a borrowed tomb before sundown (Matthew 27:57–61; Mark 15:42–47; Luke 23:50–56; John 19:38–42).

**Teaching:** Forgiveness, redemption, and fulfillment of prophecy.

## Day 8 – Saturday: In the Tomb

- Jesus rests in the tomb; guards are placed at the request of the chief priests (Matthew 27:62–66; Luke 23:56).

- Teaching: Silence before victory.

## Day 9 – Sunday: The Resurrection (Easter)

- Jesus rises early on the first day of the week (Matthew 28:1–6; Mark 16:1–6; Luke 24:1–6; John 20:1–9).

- Women discover the empty tomb; angels declare He is risen (Matthew 28:5–7).

- Jesus appears to Mary Magdalene, other women, and His disciples (Matthew 28:9–10; Luke 24:13–49; John 20).

- He commissions His disciples to preach the gospel to all nations (Matthew 28:18–20).

**Teaching:** Christ conquers death and commissions His witnesses.

This detailed timeline reflects the traditional view with a Friday crucifixion, starting from the Saturday anointing. Each day includes events, teachings, and parables as recorded, with references to harmonize the Gospel accounts.

# About the Author

Kent Merrell is a faith-fueled storyteller, entrepreneur, and unapologetic family man who believes the best adventures—whether in history books, holiday traditions, or real life—always point back to grace, grit, and a good laugh along the way.

With a career spanning four decades of crafting clever advertising copy (the kind that sells everything from widgets to wisdom), Kent now pours his energy into weaving tales that blend heart-stirring spiritual truth with page-turning drama. His historical fiction series, including The Conquest of Liberty: Moors, Monks & Monarchs and The Blade of Safavid, transports readers to epic eras of clashing empires and daring heroes, all while subtly whispering about redemption and divine purpose. But don't let the sword fights fool you—he's just as passionate about sharing his personal testimony of faith, the kind that turns ordinary days into testimonies worth telling.

In The Twelve Days of Christmas, his latest heartfelt release (hot off the press in its fresh edition), Kent dives deep into the spiritual riches hiding in those famous lyrics, inviting readers to rediscover the season's true gifts through stories, scripture, and a dash of his signature warmth.

When he's not buried in research or typing furiously, you'll find him baking up "leadership cookies"—those bite-sized nuggets of encouragement for leaders who want to guide with integrity, kindness, and maybe a little chocolate. His articles on life, love, family, and everything in between have entertained and inspired readers far and wide. (He jokes that if teaching paid the bills, he'd have spent his days in a classroom instead of a home office, shaping young minds with the same enthusiasm he now channels into books.)

At the core of it all is his deep love for family—the wife who's been his co-adventurer for decades, the five kids they've raised on stories and second helpings, and now the grandkids who keep him young (or at least pretending to be). Kent lives in Millcreek, Utah, ever grateful for the chance to testify, tell tales, and remind folks that faith isn't just serious—it's the greatest adventure of all. Grab a cookie, crack open a book, and join the journey!